CHRYSLER

Dennis Adler

Foreword by
Thomas C. Gale

MBI Publishing
Company

DEDICATION

To Jeanne, who, had she not collected Mopars, might never have come into my life. To Tom Gale for his unwavering support of this book, Steve Rossi for more reasons than I have time to list, and my friend and associate T. C. Browne, who makes me sound literate, and occasionally clever.

First published in 2000 by MBI Publishing Company,
729 Prospect Avenue, PO Box 1, Osceola, WI 54020-0001USA

MBI Publishing Company books are also available at discounts in bulk quantity for industrial or sales-promotional use. For details write to Special Sales Manager at Motorbooks International Wholesalers & Distributors, 729 Prospect Avenue, PO Box 1, Osceola WI, 54020 USA.

Library of Congress Cataloging-in-Publication Data

Adler, Dennis.
        Chrysler / Dennis Adler.
                p. cm.
        Includes index.
        ISBN 0-7603-0695-8 (hardbound : alk. paper)
        1. Chrysler Corporation–History. 2. Chrysler Automobile–History
        I. Title.
    TL215.C55 A34 2000   1999
    338.7'6292'0973–dc21
99-058170

On the front cover: A trilogy of Chrysler history covering three of the company's greatest eras. Pictured are a 1931 LeBaron-bodied Chrysler Imperial dual-cowl phaeton, a 1970 Dodge Challenger T/A, and a 1999 Dodge Viper GTS. *All vehicles courtesy DaimlerChrysler. Photographed at Meadow Brook Hall, courtesy of Oakland University*

On the frontispiece: The radiator badge and grille detail of Walter P. Chrysler's personal 1932 Imperial Speedster.

On the title page: The sweeping front fender and vented hood panel of a Ralph Roberts-designed, one-off, 1933 Chrysler LeBaron CL Sport Phaeton. In the early 1930s, when custom coachwork adorned the finest automobile chassis, a person's car became much more than a transportation device—it was a rolling work of art.

On the back cover: Memories of the past and visions of the future. From the top: a classic 1930 Imperial CG LeBaron roadster, a powerful 1958 DeSoto Adventurer, a muscular 1971 Hemi 'Cuda, and the show-stopping Chronos concept vehicle.

Edited by Keith Mathiowetz
Designed by Tom Heffron

Printed in China

CONTENTS

FOREWORD

This is a book about motor vehicles that bear the name of a man I wish I could have known—Walter P. Chrysler. It was never really a possibility, of course; he passed away before I was even born. But, years before, he had been largely responsible for the early success of General Motors' Buick division and, with it, the prosperity of my hometown of Flint, Michigan.

Today, after more than 30 years with the car company Chrysler founded in 1925, I'm indebted to him for making my *own* career possible—and more curious than ever about his life, his values, and his character.

If anything, he was decisive. As a young man, his obsession with machinery led him to early success as a machinist's apprentice with the Union Pacific Railroad—and prompted him to learn how to forge his own tools to advance his budding career. At the still-young age of 30, he had risen to become the chief mechanical officer of another Midwestern railroad. By 1910 he had become manager of a Pittsburgh locomotive manufacturing plant, only to be drawn to Flint and a managerial opportunity at Buick—at half his railroad industry salary.

Quickly, though, Chrysler's innate mechanical abilities, organizational skills, and self-confidence helped Buick become one of the most efficient producers of quality automobiles during the industry's early years. As his methods proved their worth to General Motors, Chrysler's own worth skyrocketed. By 1919 his salary was an unheard-of half-million dollars a year, allowing him to retire comfortably from GM at age 45 and embark on a second career as a savior of ailing automakers—first Willys, then Maxwell and Chalmers.

By 1923, he was ready to place his name on his own product. Working with three talented engineers, Fred Zeder, Owen Skelton and Carl Breer, he determined that he would develop a car that would establish a new standard in its field—and carry the first Chrysler badge into the marketplace.

Chrysler's directive to his engineering team was to "use the best materials adaptable to the work to be done." He expected the car to be capable of a sustained speed of 60 miles per hour, a performance standard achieved by only a few of the most expensive cars of the day. It was to be roomy enough to carry five people comfortably, economical to own and operate, and offer new standards of performance and durability.

The completed vehicle, the Chrysler Six, delivered on those promises and more. It was the first medium-priced car with a high-compression engine, a revolutionary advancement that gave the Chrysler Six greater power, torque, and efficiency than similar-sized vehicles without a corresponding increase in weight. Four-wheel hydraulic brakes, which had debuted just two years before on the Duesenberg, were also standard on the Chrysler, as were replaceable oil filters, shock absorbers, full instrumentation, windshield wipers, brake lights, rearview mirrors, and other items

available only at extra cost on competing models. For its time, the new Chrysler was also surprisingly sleek.

In late 1923, the only obstacle standing between Chrysler and his dream of volume production was financing. The upcoming 1924 New York Auto Show seemed the perfect place to introduce the Chrysler Six to the investment community, but the show was open only to cars already in production. Typical of the man, Chrysler learned which hotel would be hosting the most journalists and other influential auto show visitors, and grandly displayed the Chrysler Six in its lobby; soon he had the $5 million he needed to underwrite the car's production.

Within days the Chrysler Six was being produced in nine body styles at the Maxwell plant in Detroit and marketed through that company's national sales network. It became an instant success, and Chrysler's dream of a superior car carrying his name became a reality.

In mid-1925, Chrysler took control of Maxwell's assets, changed the company's name to the Chrysler Corporation, and never looked back. His young company not only survived the competitive warfare and daily twists and turns of the auto industry, but actually flourished in that rough-and-tumble world. Within five years of its founding, the fledgling Chrysler firm had acquired Dodge to become the third largest automobile manufacturer in America.

Chrysler's success in the automobile business followed his determination that vehicles carrying his name would set the standard of their class in performance, design, engineering, and innovation. The original Chrysler Six proved to be the perfect standard-bearer, establishing a reputation for sound engineering that would remain with the company even through the times of crushing disappointment that periodically overshadowed its years of glory. Significantly, Walter also understood—perhaps more so than others in his time—that sound design is as integral to a car's integrity as its engineering.

Looking back, it can be said that when the company fully subscribed to Chrysler's ideals—and anticipated the customer's evolving needs—it enjoyed the adulation of the car-buying public and the economic rewards that followed. When it strayed from those ideals—as it did in the late 1930s, through the postwar years, and again in the 1970s—it occasionally embraced unoriginal thinking and settled for less-challenging solutions, a certain route to decline and flirtation with failure.

Still, through the efforts of many who continued to subscribe to Walter's credo of product excellence over the years, the company was able to pull itself back to profitability, time after time. One such disciple was Virgil Exner, Chrysler's design chief in the 1950s and father of the celebrated Forward Look cars of that period.

During the postwar years, under conservative tutelage, Chrysler had continued to produce tanklike vehicles fully reflective of their prewar ancestry while competitors were developing lighter, more contemporary vehicles. To catch up, Exner began creating what he called "idea cars"—concept cars that won the hearts of potential buyers at big-city auto shows and, gradually, began to foretell the future of automotive design. Through a close working relationship with Carrozzeria Ghia in Italy, Exner developed increasingly dramatic "idea cars" until new Chrysler management and public demand combined to bring the breakthrough styling of Exner's Forward Look cars to market in the mid-1950s. Not surprisingly, sales soared.

Thirty years later—following the oil shock of the 1970s, the onset of stringent new government regulations, several periods of uncertainty

in planning, and two skirmishes with bankruptcy—Chrysler was again mired in despair. This time, those of us called upon for solutions adapted some ideas new to our industry, including the use of platform teams internally and greater component resourcing outside the company.

But, when it came to determining the form of the next generation of products, we relied heavily on the lessons of the past. We learned that it's hard to appreciate success without knowing failure—that you can find yourself quite satisfied with mediocrity if you haven't experienced the challenges presented by difficult times.

To turn Chrysler around once more, we put a significant amount of resources into breakthrough design, as Exner had done in the early 1950s. Long before we had begun to reestablish credibility in the market, we debuted significant concept cars at major auto shows, took the pulse of potential customers, then carried those lessons through to an entirely new line of head-turning production vehicles.

The very rewarding results were not unlike those enjoyed by our more successful predecessors. We quickly found that customers appreciated our willingness to take risks on their behalf in creating exciting new vehicles that stood out from the competition. Those cars generated new interest in the company, including widespread attention from younger buyers who had previously never considered a Chrysler. Once again, Walter Chrysler's convictions were underscored. Chrysler employees were again justifiably proud of the products their company was creating—and, once again, customers returned in record numbers.

To me, these experiences do not merely typify Chrysler's feast-or-famine existence over the past 75 years; instead, they help explain the recurring and deep-rooted affection of millions for the company occasionally dismissed by some journalists as being merely "the *smallest* of the Big Three automakers."

The Chrysler faithful know that no business survives three-quarters of a century without some inherent good. They understand that economic times have perhaps ebbed and flowed more frequently and more dramatically for Chrysler than for other automakers. But they also know that Chrysler vehicles speak for themselves without hesitation or apology—and to the times that produced them.

My greatest regret is that I can't take Walter Chrysler on a tour of today's DaimlerChrysler design studios—that I can't show him the vehicles of the future, ask his opinions, or thank him for creating the organization and maintaining the ideals responsible for the vehicles depicted in this book. In my view, the 75 years of automotive history charted here represent an extraordinary record of achievement—and serve as a model for an even more remarkable future.

Enjoy the journey—past and present—in the pages that follow.

Thomas C. Gale
Executive Vice President
Chrysler Product Strategy and Design, and General Manager
Passenger Car Operations,
DaimlerChrysler Corporation

ACKNOWLEDGMENTS

In most cases when I write a book, it is about a company that has long since shuttered its doors. It therefore becomes a search for historic data, old photos, a hunt, if you will, for the remaining pieces of a puzzle that is rarely ever complete.

This time I have been blessed with a book about a company that not only is still in business but at the very top of its game. And I have been doubly blessed with the support of one of that company's top executives, Thomas C. Gale, who has been behind this project since its inception early in 1998, nearly six months before the merger with Daimler-Benz AG. That event changed the course of this book, which was to have been in celebration of Chrysler Corporation's 75th anniversary in June 2000 an event that will never officially take place, since Chrysler Corporation, as a separate entity, no longer exists. Thus, in its place, we pay tribute to 75 years of the Chrysler marque and the companies which have become part of the Chrysler fold over the past three-quarters of a century.

Through the support of Tom Gale, Chrysler Corporation Public Relations, the Walter P. Chrysler Museum, and the Chrysler Historical Foundation, I have had access to one of the most complete historical archives ever compiled by any automaker. No amount of thanks can ever express my gratitude to the men and women of Chrysler Corporation for their help. There are, however, many whose efforts must be acknowledged. DaimlerChrysler Executive Vice President Tom Gale; Steve Rossi, Vice President DaimlerChrysler Global Product Communications; Rita McKay, Director, Walter P. Chrysler Museum; Barry Dressel, Manager, Walter P. Chrysler Museum; Chrysler automotive collection curator Brandt Rosenbusch; Barbara Fronczak, Senior Manager, Chrysler Historical Foundation; Otto Rosenbusch; Don Sommer; John McMullin; Frank Kleptz, David Kleptz, and Ryan Kleptz; Jeff Ring; Joan and Octie Ham; Lisa Baylis Ashby; Meadow Brook Hall and Oakland University in Rochester, Michigan; T. C. Browne; and all of the Chrysler, Dodge, and Plymouth owners who were kind enough to make their cars available for this book.

My sincere thanks and appreciation to one and all.
—Dennis Adler

INTRODUCTION

Strange though it may sound, the merger of Chrysler Corporation with Daimler-Benz AG in November 1998, just 14 months shy of the Detroit automaker's 75th anniversary, was simply another step in a long progression of events set into motion more than a century ago.

It began with one of the most complex stories in the history of the U.S. motor industry, the rise and fall of Colonel Albert A. Pope's turn-of-the-century automotive empire, which included the successful Pope-Toledo and Pope-Hartford gasoline cars, and an electric car known as the Columbia or Pope-Columbia.

Walter P. Chrysler's 1932 Imperial Speedster was a one-of-a-kind design built on the short 135-inch CH wheelbase instead of the Imperial Custom's 146-inch platform, which made the lengthy Imperial hood appear even longer. After a complete restoration in 1990 by current owner Sam Mann, the car went on to win Best of Show at the 1991 Pebble Beach Concours d'Elegance.

Walter P. Chrysler (at right) with Chrysler distributor Carl Wallerich and the 1926 Imperial 80 chosen as the pacesetter for that year's Indianapolis 500 mile race.

market for gas-, steam-, and electric-powered vehicles. The horse was still king of the road.

In 1901, Col. Pope's empire dealt itself a trump card with the purchase of the famed Selden patent, a clever little work of legal legerdemain that in essence granted Pope exclusive rights to the manufacture of gasoline-powered automobiles in the U.S. Thus, every automaker in the country would, in theory, have to pay a royalty to Pope for licensing rights. What irked everyone, except Pope, was that G. B. Selden, who filed for and received patent No. 549,160 on November 5, 1895, never built a production automobile until 1907. George Baldwin Selden, an inventor and patent attorney, simply drew up the plans and patented the idea. After Pope purchased the rights to Selden's patent, he went after every automaker in the country producing a vehicle powered by an internal combustion engine. And it worked until 1910, when Henry Ford finally had his fill of it and took Selden and Pope to court, proving that the patent was unenforceable. The gravy train that had been running directly into Pope's coffers was abruptly derailed in January 1911, when the court ruled in Ford's favor. For the first time in a decade, the Pope empire had to take a long look at its profitability solely from the manufacturing of motorcars, which at the time, turned out to be the least of its problems.

By 1897, just two years after the first Columbia electrics were shown, the first of many mergers was in the works. One of Pope's divisions became the Columbia Automobile Company of Hartford, Connecticut, which also included the Electric Vehicle Company of Hartford, registered in 1897 with $12 million capital. The company was run by former U.S. Secretary of the Navy W. C. Whitney, who used Col. Pope's assembly plants for most of his requirements, including the fulfillment of an order for 1,600 electric taxi cabs in 1899. For a brief period, Hartford became the automotive capital of America, and by 1907 some 9,000 of the battery-powered taxis operating in the eastern United States, including Washington, D.C., were built by Columbia.

Pope became one of the nation's leading manufacturers by the turn of the century, and one of the first to place the engine of his gasoline-powered models ahead of the driver (rather than behind or beneath the seat), and the first to offer a steering wheel (up to this time steering was by a tiller).

The Pope combine stumbled along in the first few years of the twentieth century as competition grew from emerging automakers in Indiana, Ohio, New York, and Michigan. The American automotive industry was evolving and growing at a much faster pace than the

Walter Chrysler proudly introduced the all-new Chrysler in 1924. This is the first car built, a two-door brougham.

In 1934, the 123-inch-wheelbase Model CU Airflow four-door sedan with seating for six passengers sold for only $1,345. This model had the highest production run of the year, 7,226 examples compared to 732 of the five-passenger coupes, 306 brougham coupes, and 125 town sedans.

Two years before the Selden patent reached the end of the road, Col. Pope had passed away at the age of 66, and his brother George had taken over the day-to-day operations. Electric Vehicle had renamed itself the Columbia Motor Car Company, and in 1910 it became embroiled in Benjamin Brisco's United States Motors Corporation debacle, a failed attempt to build a conglomerate of independent companies to rival William C. Durant's General Motors. The collapse of the U.S. Motors combine in 1912 not only brought an end to Columbia; it also took down partners Brush (founded by the talented automotive engineer Alanson P. Brush), Stoddard-Dayton, and Brisco's own company, Maxwell-Brisco (founded in 1905 and financed in part by millionaire J. P. Morgan). Pope also fell into receivership shortly after, and by 1914 was defunct.

The only marque to survive United States Motors Corporation was Maxwell, which within a year was resurrected by Ben Brisco's former associate, automotive engineer Jonathan Maxwell. With new production facilities in Detroit, the company prospered until the post–World War I recession in 1920. Two years later the

The sporty Town & Country convertible introduced in 1946 launched Chrysler into the postwar era with a winning combination of style and performance. Even with the top up, the car still retained a sleek profile.

The bold, Exner-designed 300C grille, flanked by quad headlights, gave the car an enormous head-on profile. The intense styling of the 300C really stands out on this jet black car. Other colors for 1957 included cloud white, Gauguin red, parade green, and copper brown.

grim reaper was knocking on Maxwell's door and the only way out appeared to be a page from U.S. Motors' shadowy past—a merger. The best suitor appeared to be another struggling Detroit automaker with which Maxwell had already allied itself in 1921, Chalmers. Founded in 1908 by Hugh Chalmers, vice president of the National Cash Register Company, and engineers Howard Coffin and Roy Chapin (who went on to launch Hudson in 1910 with department store tycoon

Joseph L. Hudson), Chalmers was in even worse shape than Maxwell. Late in 1922 the two foundering companies joined forces to form Maxwell-Chalmers, now one foundering company.

Back in 1921, Walter P. Chrysler had been approached by the Maxwell and Chalmers board of directors to step in and resuscitate the impoverished companies, both of which were on the brink of receivership. By 1923 Walter Chrysler had turned Maxwell around, and

the fate of Chalmers hung in the balance. It was to be the final year for the marque. In 1924 a new Maxwell model, called the Chrysler, made its debut, and in June 1925, Maxwell was reorganized as the Chrysler Corporation.

With what was primarily a high-end product line, Walter Chrysler decided to venture into Ford and Chevrolet's territory in 1928, launching both the lower-priced Plymouth and DeSoto brands to complement the luxurious Chrysler and Imperial models. He then purchased Dodge Brothers, adding Dodge cars and trucks to the expanding Chrysler Corporation. At the time, the purchase of Dodge was the largest automotive merger in American automotive history.

A decade later, Walter P. Chrysler retired as chairman of the company bearing his name, and when he died at age 65, on August 18, 1940, it was with the confidence that he had created a company that in just 15 years had grown into the third largest automaker in America. His friend

Taking up the mantle of the legendary Chrysler letter cars, the 2000 Chrysler 300M delivers exceptional four-door family car styling fused with sports coupe performance in a twenty-first century vogue.

The 'Cuda's stablemate at Dodge was the Challenger R/T. Aimed at a slightly different market segment than the 'Cuda, Dodge was after the Cougar crowd, while the 'Cuda was looking to take a bite out of Mustang and Camaro Z-28 sales. The sportiest R/T model (R/T for Road/Track) was the hemi-powered convertible.

Affordable and a street-worthy competitor with more costly muscle cars, the 1970 Plymouth Road Runner was one of Chrysler Corporation's best sellers. Sales for the model totaled 43,404.

Major Edward Bowes, who hosted the weekly radio show *Major Bowes Amateur Hour*, said of Chrysler, "He was an American workman—industrial giant—a truly great gentlemen. Walter Chrysler's monument is the business he founded to be carried on by men of genius of his own choosing—groomed by him for the inevitable task—and schooled in his inspirational methods."

Chrysler's opinion of himself was far less grandiose. He was by nature a humble man. In his 1937 autobiography, *Life of an American Workman*, Walter Chrysler wrote: "I got my start in overalls; so did Zeder; so did Hutchinson; so did Skelton; so did Breer; so did Byron Foy; as did many others. We are . . . American workmen in the simple, exact meaning of the term. Those who come after us in the years ahead will be the same, and the reason for this is that there is no other way for men to qualify for what we do . . . except by work and learning."

What Walter P. Chrysler could never have imagined was the direction that his work, his company, and the men who would follow in his footsteps would take in the decades to come.

The merger of all mergers, or so it seemed at the time, came in 1987 when Chrysler Corporation purchased American Motors Corporation. This brought so many historic names into the Chrysler fold, that aside from net worth, Chrysler was bigger than General Motors. With the acquisition of AMC, Chrysler now owned Jeep as well as all of the surviving American Motors products.

AMC had itself been formed by a 1954 merger between Hudson and Nash, which also included Willys (Jeep), and the individual marques that had come under the Hudson and Nash banners over the years, including Kaiser, Frazier, Willys-Overland, and Graham. After the AMC acquisition, it was as though a great agglomeration of American automotive history had been compressed into one entity, the Chrysler Corporation.

When one considers the remarkable accomplishments of Chrysler Corporation during the reign of Lee Iacocca, who held the company together during its darkest period, Bob Lutz, who guided Chrysler into a new era of design and engineering, and current chairman Robert J. Eaton, men all cut from the same dynamic cloth as Walter P. Chrysler, it seems baffling that at a time when the company was producing the best-built, best-styled, and best-selling cars and trucks in its entire history, a merger would even be considered. But that is exactly the kind of move that has characterized Chrysler Corporation since its founding. It is interesting to note that the three largest mergers in the history of the American automobile industry have all involved Chrysler.

Over the past decade Chrysler has raised the benchmark for American automotive styling higher than any other automaker. From a company that was once considered stodgy and out of step, Chrysler has reinvented itself as a forward-thinking, and some would say, risk-taking automaker, that has put itself on the cutting edge of design. In 2000 there isn't a conservative body style in the entire Chrysler lineup.

Chrysler Executive Vice President Thomas C. Gale notes, "One of the things that made Chrysler such a strong merger candidate in some respects was design. We improved the equity, certainly the market cap of our company to the point where one of the most prestigious marques in the world would want to be associated and joined with us. That's a real credit to everybody who works at Chrysler." Even this is not uncharacteristic of Chrysler if one looks back throughout the company's history. In 1925, the Imperial was a high-water mark in

luxury car design. In the 1930s, the Airflow, though unsuccessful commercially, blazed a new trail in automobile design, taking aerodynamics from theory to practice. In the 1950s, Chrysler chief stylist Virgil Exner created cars that simply stunned the Detroit establishment and left buyers breathless with high-performance models like the Chrysler 300C. In the late 1960s and early 1970s, Chrysler redefined the musclecar with the Hemi 'Cuda, Road Runner, Dodge Scat Pack, and Plymouth Rapid Transit System. And in the 1990s the men and women of Chrysler have simply left the rest of the automotive world in their wake with aggressively styled cars, sporty four-door family sedans that can be recognized as Chrysler products a block away, sports cars like the Viper GTS ACR and Prowler that have no equal in the American marketplace, and trucks and minivans that have set new standards for sport utility and recreational vehicles.

It was as historically certain as Walter Chrysler's acquisition of Dodge more than 60 years ago, that Chrysler Corporation would one day merge with another major automaker. It is therefore no surprise that Daimler-Benz and Chrysler have become one. It is a new beginning for the world's oldest car company and the world's most innovative, a marriage not of convenience, nor of necessity, but of mutual admiration.

That is something Walter P. Chrysler could understand.

Performance was sneaking into Chrysler products through turbocharging. The 1986 LeBaron GTS got a boost to its 2.2-liter four-cylinder engine from a Chrysler turbo and fuel injection. The cars were priced at $11,437.

CHAPTER 1

WALTER P. CHRYSLER

You call this retiring?

Walter Chrysler was always fascinated by machines. In 1908, before he had even learned to drive, he purchased, disassembled, and then reassembled a brand new Locomobile touring car. Chrysler was 33 years old, and had yet to begin his career in the automotive world. At the time, he was the superintendent of the Chicago Great Western Railroad.

"I loved to see the engines with their mysteries exposed. I envied the mechanics who understood their inner workings," wrote Chrysler of his early days as a sweeper in the Union Pacific Railroad machine shop. That was in the spring of 1892 when he was but 18 years old.

Eager to indulge his curiosity, he began a four-year apprenticeship in the Union Pacific machine shop. In 1897 he made his first career move, leaving the Union Pacific for a better position with the Atchison, Topeka & Santa Fe Railroad in Wellington, Kansas. But his time there was brief. His desire to

Walter P. Chrysler was a man of vision, whether building cars or erecting skyscrapers.

Amid the Manhattan skyline of the 1930s, the Chrysler Building was a shining jewel.
Photographed in 1930 by Irving Browning, his historic panorama shows the Daily News, Chrysler, and Chanin buildings.
Collection of The New York Historical Society

take on new challenges, which manifested itself as a kind of bright-eyed wanderlust, drove him to move from one job to the next, back to the Union Pacific, then on to Denver for a job with the Colorado & Southern Railroad. In 1900 he decided to settle down in Salt Lake City, Utah, working for the Denver & Rio Grande Western Railroad. A year later he married his hometown sweetheart, Della Forker, who had been waiting faithfully for him in Ellis, Kansas. Della joined Walter in Salt Lake, where he had been promoted to the position of roundhouse foreman.

A few years later the Chrysler family—Walter, Della, and their first child, Thelma—picked up and relocated to Trinidad, Colorado, where he took a job with a former employer, the Colorado & Southern. That lasted less than a year before Walter uprooted his family once more and headed south to Texas for assignment as a master mechanic with the Fort Worth & Denver Railroad in Childress, a one-horse town that didn't even have the horse.

Life in Texas was hard, and in less than a year another offer came Walter's way. The best ever. It was from the Chicago Great Western Railroad, which wanted him to come east and take a position as master mechanic. Within two years Walter Chrysler was superintendent of motive power for the entire railroad.

This could have been the end of the Chrysler story, but by chance, Chrysler's boss—a man who took little

notice of the countless hours Chrysler put in traveling the rails to ensure that everything was running smoothly—questioned him as to why one of the trains had been late. When Chrysler, who had been traveling for more than a week inspecting the lines, said he would look into it first thing, the man, as Walter later recalled in his autobiography, "started to wail and moan at me." Chrysler reached into his pocket and withdrew a billfold swelling with the railroad passes he had used the previous week riding the trains from town to town on his inspection tour, and promptly flung it down upon the man's desk, the indignation in his eyes as clear as his conviction to walk out the door and never return. "That is how I became an ex-railroad man," wrote Chrysler.

Mechanical ability and organizational skills were not necessarily limited to working on the railroad, and Chrysler, still intrigued with the Locomobile he had purchased, decided to look into the automotive industry. He landed on the doorstep of the troubled American Locomotive Company in Pittsburgh, Pennsylvania, maker of the very expensive and luxurious ALCO motorcar. He was put in charge of the Allegheny plant, which was streaming red ink, and inside of a year he had turned the operation into a profit maker. Walter P. Chrysler had salvaged his first auto company.

In 1912 he went to work for the Buick Division of General Motors, moving his family once again, which now included an infant son, Jack, born just before the move from Pittsburgh, Pennsylvania, to Flint, Michigan. This was the same year Buick boss Charlie Nash became president of General Motors, beginning a long imbroglio with William C. Durant and the GM board of directors for control of the company Durant had founded.

When Durant regained control of GM in 1915, Charlie Nash decided it was time to take his leave, after a year of countless disputes. In 1917 he founded the Nash motor car company in Kenosha, Wisconsin. Chrysler, who was momentarily in Durant's favor, was offered the presidency of Buick, at the then unheard of salary of $500,000 a year.

The relationship between Walter Chrysler and Billy Durant was amicable at best, confrontational at its worst, and after three years Chrysler withdrew his metaphorical billfold full of rail passes and flung it on Durant's desk. He never looked back. Chrysler had fully intended to retire at that moment. Having amassed a fortune at GM in salary and stock options, there was little reason for him to seek other employment. However,

it sought him out, and within months he was on the payroll at Willys-Overland, to oversee the New York automaker's reorganization.

Walter P. Chrysler never retired. He saved Willys, turned Maxwell into the Chrysler Corporation in 1925, and worked almost every day until ill health forced him to turn company management over to Chrysler President K. T. Keller in 1938.

THE CHRYSLER BUILDING

The Great War of 1914–1918 had been a good deal easier on the United States than it had on the nations of Eastern and Western Europe. The Doughboys came marching home to the best brass bands available, there were jobs for heroes, and it would take only a couple of years of postwar business decline before the great cycle of economic growth began what was to become known affectionately as the Roaring Twenties.

New York City found itself crowded with enterprises needing to grow and little room for them to grow. Tall buildings were no strangers to the city, but never before had the demand for office space been so great and financing so available. Once the money was arranged—generally by bond issue—the soaring, new commercial

The most popular building in New York City (sorry, Empire State Building and World Trade Center), the Chrysler Building has been featured in more movies and television commercials than any other. A favorite of science fiction film directors and cinematographers, the stainless-steel-clad dome has been toppled in such recent films as *Armageddon*, *Independence Day*, and *Godzilla*. Seems there's nothing quite like the camera's point of view at street level as the spire comes plunging earthward. The photo was taken in 1930 by Irving Browning. *Collection of the New York Historical Society*

Chryslers were mostly conservative in styling, and the Chrysler Imperial Sedan, priced at $1,895, was very limited in production the first year. The companion model was the Crown Imperial Sedan at $2,195, which featured a stylish cameo window in the rear, rather than a full-size window, as shown on this 1924 Imperial Sedan from the Nethercutt Collection.

One of the displays at the Walter P. Chrysler Museum, in Auburn Hills, Michigan, re-creates Walter P. Chrysler's workshop. Many of the items used in the re-creation were Chrysler's original tools.

buildings of central Manhattan would indeed be constructed, by some architect, for some client, some time.

The race for the sky was kicked off by a proposal for the Larkin Tower, a monster designed to hold 30,000 office workers, in a telescopic shaft that would rise 1,208 feet, with 110 stories of offices, enclosing 950,000 square feet of rentable floor space, all on 50,000 square feet of dirt.

The Larkin Tower offended many, pleased few, and was never built; but it did inspire others to step up to the plate and swing. Among these were three firms of architects, all charged up with skyscraper fever, and determined to be the first to create the world's tallest structure, a distinction owned at the time by the Eiffel Tower at a height of 1,024 feet.

One challenger was the Bank of Manhattan Company Building, designed by the architecture firm of H. Craig Severance & Yasuo Matsui. Another was a project for William H. Reynolds, one-time member of the New York State Senate and not-always-successful speculator in real estate and entertainment facilities, the most famous having been "Dreamland" at Coney Island.

Reynolds, who liked to be called "Senator," retained William van Alen, who had recently terminated a partnership with the above mentioned H. Craig Severance.

When "Senator" Reynolds ran out of chips, Walter P. Chrysler took over Reynolds' plan and van Alen's designs, changing little but adding details that would exploit the structure to herald the visible virtues of Chrysler Corporation vehicles. He also instructed the architect to increase the building's height to 925 feet and add some strong automotive reminders of where the money had come from.

Then, William van Alen challenged J. E. R. Carpenter, architect of the Lincoln Building, to a duel of the stories, as it were: Carpenter had announced the Lincoln Building would rise to 55; van Alen proclaimed the Chrysler Building would be 56. Carpenter countered with 63; van Alen announced a 65-story Chrysler Building. As

it turned out, Carpenter had just been fooling around, and the Lincoln Building rose to a paltry 55 floors.

But van Alen was by no means out of the woods; his parting with Severance had been on less than jolly terms and each announced that his new building would be the world's tallest. While this rivalry was blooming, Walter P. Chrysler ordered van Alen to reduce the height of the Chrysler Building by 10 floors and—caught up in the excitement—shortly reversed himself.

His architect, meanwhile, added more floors to keep the heat on, only to discover, in the winter of 1929, that Severance had received permission to add a lantern at the top of the Bank of Manhattan Company Building. He also decided to add a 50-foot flagpole as well.

It looked as if Severance had won the improbable contest. History does not record the fascinating details of the van Alen/Chrysler plot, but what else could it have been? Surely, Mr. Chrysler must have been aware of what van Alen was up to: he had concealed a 185-foot spire in the upper reaches of his creation, not to be revealed until Severance had topped out the Bank of Manhattan Company Building at 71 stories plus 927 feet, a total that would have exceeded the published altitude of the Chrysler Building by 24 inches!

But it didn't. In one of the best-kept secrets in the long history of architecture, and a wildly successful engineering achievement, William van Alen had designed an art deco stepped-dome crown clad in Nircosta metal and stored it in pieces on the 65th floor of the nearly completed building. Nircosta is a stainless alloy, strong as steel and glossy like platinum; this was the first use of this metal in building construction.

Almost to the second after his rival's skyscraper topped out in November 1929, van Alen gave the signal. Machinery started to growl, and silver panels began to grow out of what the sophisticated New York street audience had supposed was the building's upper limit. As they gaped like country bumpkins, the panels continued to grow, and—in about 90 minutes—the top of the building was finally riveted in place, soaring 1,046 feet skyward, the tallest man-made structure in the world!

Walter P. Chrysler had van Alen incorporate sculptures of automobile motifs in the exterior design, the most striking of which are the menacing gargoyles stationed at four corners of the structure, and said to have been modeled after the 1929 Plymouth hood ornament. Elsewhere, there are replicas of road wheel hubcaps, but these features are hardly visible from the street.

In somber contrast to the towering elegance of the main structure, are the street-level entrances. The main one is on Lexington Avenue, the other two open out onto 42nd and 43rd streets. Chrysler and van Alen spared no expense in the effort to impress the other architects and automobile tycoons, decorating the interior with red Moroccan marble walls and yellow Siena marble floors; all of the building's 32 elevators had magnificent art deco treatments done in rare wood marquetry. No possibility to dazzle the proletariat had been overlooked, from the lobby's 100x75-foot ceiling mural, to the building's Oz-like pinnacle 1,046 feet above the street.

The 77-story Chrysler building opened its doors in April 1930. The original "business" purpose of the structure--a New York headquarters for the Chrysler Corporation--never matured, however. Before World War II, there was a showroom, with Chrysler vehicles in all their waxed and polished splendor located in the lobby. Whether one could actually buy an automobile off that floor is lost to fading memories.

Inside the spire, a properly appointed luxury apartment, with triangular windows, was installed for the person whose name the building bears. Since Prohibition had not yet run its annoying course, there was a males-only retreat known as the Cloud Club, with lockers for one's favorite tipple and coded identification in case the feds should bust in.

According to the legend, Walter P. Chrysler locked his apartment for the last time the day the Empire State Building topped out higher than the Chrysler Building.

The building was sold long ago, and currently belongs to Tishman Speyer Properties, but it still serves as a positive icon to the memory of Walter P. Chrysler and the company he founded.

The 1928 Chrysler 72 Sport Roadster was priced at $1,525. A limited production model introduced late in the year, the cars came equipped with cowl lights and chromed headlights.

CHAPTER 2

WALTER P. AT THE HELM

The founding of the Chrysler Corporation

Walter Percy Chrysler built the company bearing his name by salvaging the bankrupt Maxwell-Chalmers concern—which was all but done for when he signed on as chairman of the Reorganization and Management Committee in 1921. The "company doctor," as Chrysler had come to be known around Detroit, was already involved in restoring the debt-burdened Willys-Overland Company to solvency when he was called upon by Maxwell. Within two years, the retired GM executive vice president and former head of the Buick Division had restored the company to profitability, and by 1924 had doubled production, converting the automaker's stream of red ink into earnings of $2.6 million. Chrysler had also reincorporated Maxwell-Chalmers as the Maxwell Motors Corporation, with himself as chairman, the first in a stunning series of corporate maneuvers that

In 1928 Chrysler introduced a Sport Roadster equipped with an 85-horsepower six known as the "Red Head." The car pictured, owned by Gene Cofer of Tucker, Georgia, is painted in the original Sport Roadster color scheme advertised in 1928 of thorn brown, Moorish brown and orange. It is also equipped with the optional wire wheels and sidemounts.

The Chrysler emblem from the 1920s was a grand design; so much so, that Chrysler replaced its pentastar trademark in 1995 with the original crest.

Among the most stylish of early Chrysler Imperial designs was the 1928 Touralette. The original was a one-off design penned by stylist John Tjaarda. The coachbuilding firm of Locke obtained the rights from Tjaarda, and 21 additional cars were produced on the Imperial 80 chassis. Among several outstanding features are scalloped molding that runs completely around the body, and finely detailed cane work on the entire rear portion of the car.

would eventually give him controlling interest. Around Detroit people were already starting to call the company Maxwell-Chrysler, after Chalmers did a quiet fade to black at the end of the 1924 model year.

A MANAGER'S MANAGER

In March 1920, Walter Chrysler had retired as Vice President of General Motors, where he was earning more than $500,000 a year. But in truth it was a resignation of his own choosing to underscore his disapproval of William C. Durant's management decisions. Chrysler had strongly voiced his disapproval of Durant's overly aggressive expansion programs, and constant meddling in the Buick Division, which Chrysler had been running profitably since 1917. He believed that Durant's actions would lead GM to disaster. As it turned out, Billy Durant only led himself to disaster, when he was finally ousted from GM for the second and last time in 1920. By then, however, Chrysler had taken his leave and signed on at Willys-Overland.

At Maxwell, Walter P. had worked his magic with sales, marketing, and engineering, just as he had at Willys, his salvage operation at the company's New York headquarters completed in the fall of 1922. It had taken him just two years to turn the financially ailing Willys-Overland concern around, and he had been paid the

The standard Chrysler Imperial engine for 1928 was increased to 309 cubic inches; it developed 100 horsepower. The cars were capable of a top speed of 80 miles per hour.

tured a 68-horsepower, 201.5-cubic-inch high-compression L-head engine with aluminum pistons, detachable cylinder head, vacuum fuel feed, full-pressure lubrication, seven-bearing crankshaft, carburetor air cleaner, and a replaceable element oil filter. The car was also the first in its price class to come equipped with Lockheed four-wheel hydraulic brakes. Starting at just $1,335, the Chrysler B-70 was the most automobile anyone had yet offered for the money, an honest rival to such long established marques as Auburn, Buick, Studebaker, and Nash, all offering six-cylinder power, but none with the combination of features available on the new 1924 Chrysler.

The year following the Chrysler's introduction, Walter Chrysler made a bold move that would change the very future of the American automotive industry. Mustering all of his financial resources, which included substantial stock holdings in General Motors, he amassed as much capital as possible, including some $15 million in bank-funded loans, which he used to purchase all of Maxwell's assets. Maxwell's shareholders not only approved of this but agreed to exchange their stock in Maxwell for shares in Chrysler, thus allowing the reorganization of Maxwell as the Chrysler Corporation on June 26, 1925. The next morning Maxwell ceased to exist.

In less than five years, Walter Chrysler had taken a nearly bankrupt company and turned it into one of the crown jewels of the American automotive industry. Chrysler Corporation earned $17 million in 1925 on sales of more than 130,000 cars, and by year's end, there were more than 3,800 dealers selling Chrysler automobiles from coast to coast.

In 1926 another 162,242 cars rolled off the assembly lines, moving Chrysler into the number five spot in industry sales. Spearheading Chrysler's drive to expand into the luxury car market was the luxurious new Chrysler Imperial E-80, introduced in January at the National Automobile Show. The new model was available in six standard body styles: roadster, coupe, phaeton, five- and seven-passenger sedans, and seven-passenger limousine, all on a standard 120-inch-wheelbase chassis. Two long-wheelbase chassis, 127-inch and 133-inch, were also available with custom coachwork in landaulet or town car styling.

All Imperial models were powered by a larger and more powerful seven-main bearing Chrysler L-head six. With a bore and stroke of 3 1/2x5 inches, displacement was 288 cubic inches, with a 92-horsepower output.

princely sum of $2 million for his efforts. Maxwell, however, was another story. He had accepted a trifling $100,000 a year salary and stock options for his efforts. Between 1921 and 1924 Walter Chrysler had done more than merely stem the flow of red ink. He had reinvented Maxwell and made it his own.

The first public indication of Chrysler's intentions came in 1924, when the company introduced a new model bearing the Chrysler name. Just as Henry Ford, Ransom E. Olds, David Dunbar Buick, Charles Nash, and John and Horace Dodge had done before him, Walter P. Chrysler had made the car and the car company one and the same, giving it an identity that could be easily associated by consumers with an individual, rather than a faceless conglomerate. Under his stewardship, Maxwell Motors sold nearly 80,000 cars in 1924, and of that total, 32,000 bore the Chrysler signature.

The new models, which had been designed by Walter Chrysler's personal engineering staff, composed of Carl Breer, Fred Zeder, and Owen Skelton (who had first worked with Chrysler at Willys-Overland), was brimming with innovations never before offered on a medium-priced, six-cylinder car. The new Chrysler fea-

Positioned right below the Imperial line in 1929, the Model 75 Tonneau Phaeton was the most luxurious midpriced model offered by Chrysler. A dual-cowl design, the car had a particularly sporty look with both windshields lowered. It was priced at $1,835; only 227 examples were built in 1929.

The smaller Chrysler G70 six had a swept volume of 218.6 cubic inches and delivered 68 horsepower. Both Chrysler lines used a three-speed manual transmission.

The Imperial name had originally been selected by Walter Chrysler to designate an individual body style, rather than a series of cars, and had been offered in two versions in 1924—Imperial and Crown Imperial (another distinctive name that would resurface years later within the Chrysler line). Distinguishing the Crown Imperial was a half-roof covered in leather or fabric and characterized by a small cameo window, an elegant, oval-shaped portal positioned just behind the rear door glass.

Beginning in 1926 the Imperial became an individual line, and the "80" designation represented more than just a new model: the Imperial 80 was guaranteed to reach a top speed of no less than 80 miles per hour—an astonishingly high speed for the roads of the day. Most of the coachwork for the Imperial line was designed

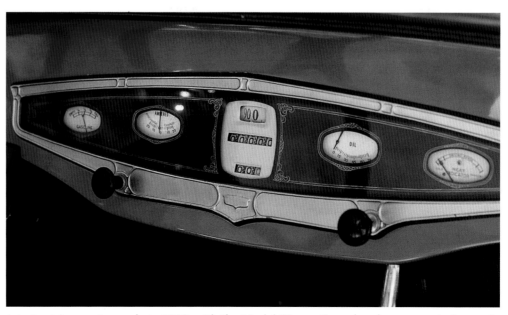

Interior trim went upscale in 1929, with the Model 75 sporting a handsome new instrument panel done in ebony black with gold trim, surrounded by a beautifully cast metal fascia.

Locke turned out to be one of Chrysler's more popular coachbuilders in the late 1920s, producing such striking semicustoms as this sporty rumble seat roadster with speedster styling. The sweptback body lines were accented by a folding windshield and stylish two-tone paint scheme. *Chrysler Historical Foundation*

either by Ralph Roberts of LeBaron Carrossier, or LeBaron's renowned cofounder, Raymond Dietrich.

By 1926 Walter Chrysler and Ray Dietrich had become friends and were routinely getting together for what Dietrich later described as "Saturday afternoons at the two-bit lunch counter, where Walter and I ate frankfurters washed down with beer and discussed new design programs." That same year Dietrich decided to leave LeBaron and open his own design firm in partnership with the Murray Body Corporation of Detroit—then the largest supplier of sheet metal stampings in the auto

The Plymouth PB "College Special," priced at just $595, could be painted to order in the color scheme of your favorite college. This PB is part of the Frank Kleptz collection.

industry. The plan had been to make Dietrich Inc. the custom body division of Murray. Dietrich, however, chose to distance himself from the parent company, which was having financial problems, moving instead into a separate building near the Packard factory on East Grand Boulevard. Although the move was intended to put him closer to Alvan Macauley, who had hired Dietrich as a styling consultant for Packard in 1925, Dietrich's principal client became Edsel Ford and the Lincoln Motor Company, which had helped fund the recapitalization of Murray. Still, the ever industrious Ray Dietrich managed to work both sides of the street, in a manner of speaking, and in addition to designing cars for Lincoln, developed a new series of exclusive semicustom designs for Packard, while also penning new styles for Chrysler! This was one reason why Dietrich virtually dominated automobile styling throughout the late 1920s, and well into the 1930s. In 1934, however, Walter Chrysler finally persuaded him to get a steady job, and Dietrich became head of the Chrysler styling department, where he would remain until 1938.

Between Dietrich and Ralph Roberts at LeBaron (which had become part of the Briggs Body Company with principal operations in Detroit), Walter P. had his hand on the very pulse of American automotive styling, and he had the cars and the sales to prove it. Chrysler Imperials were ranked among the best engineered and most attractively styled automobiles in the nation, and in the minds of most consumers they were the equal of Cadillac, Lincoln, and Packard in every respect.

WHAT'S IN A NAME

The first production cars to bear the Chrysler name had been the 1924 Series B70. When the Imperial was introduced in 1926, the newer G70 became Chrysler's midpriced line. (The Maxwell had also been replaced in 1926 by a new lower-priced Chrysler, the Model 58, which sold for $890 and was powered by a redesigned Maxwell 185-cubic-inch, 38-horsepower, four-cylinder engine.) The 70 remained in production for another year after the Imperial's debut, finally being succeeded by the improved Chrysler 72 in 1928.

The new Chrysler 72 models were powered by either a standard six-cylinder, 248.9-cubic-inch Silver Dome engine, or the optional 85-horsepower Red Head engine with Invarstrut pistons, a higher 6.2:1 compression ratio, dual point distributor, and enlarged intake manifold. The series numbers used by Chrysler were

Although Plymouth was competitive with the Ford Model A and Chevrolet Model AB, in 1929 Chevy upped the ante by equipping the all-new Model AC with a six-cylinder engine and a base price some $145 less than the Plymouth's. Being a Chrysler product, however, gave Plymouth a greater perceived value. The sporty Plymouth models were still packing four-cylinder engines up through 1932, but that allowed them to sell for less than most competitive makes. In 1932 Plymouth moved up to the number three sales spot in America, ahead of Buick and Pontiac, but still lagging behind Ford and Chevrolet.

Plymouth interiors were simple but well designed.

The DeSoto (after explorer Hernando DeSoto, who discovered the Mississippi—"*Santo vaca, that's a lot of water!*") gave Chrysler a second lower-priced model and essentially a companion to the Plymouth. Both lines shared many of the same components for chassis, driveline, and bodies. The DeSotos, however, came equipped with a six-cylinder engine, rather than a four. The most successful new model launch of the 1920s, DeSoto produced more than 80,000 cars during its first year. The example pictured is a 1932 SC Victoria Coupe from the Frank Kleptz collection.

again chosen to reflect the top speed that each model could attain. "It is named the '72'—with the assurance of 72 and more miles per hour whenever you will."

The Series 72 Sport Roadster proved to be Chrysler's "hot rod" for the 1928 model year, and the only year in which this specific version was built. The 1928 Chryslers, all-new from the chassis up, rode on a 120.5-inch wheelbase platform with solid axles front and rear and exceptionally long leaf springs of silico-manganese steel. The "72" models were fitted with 30x6-inch tires mounted to either standard wood wheels or optional wire spoke wheels, and featured four-wheel outside contracting hydraulic brakes, rated at the time among the best in the industry.

Added after the new model year had begun, the Sport Roadster differed in a number of features including an extra panel under the belt line, matching colored fenders, chromed headlamps, cowl lights, the Red Head engine as standard equipment, and a price some $100 higher than the Roadster, which started at $1,495. For the entire model year, Chrysler produced a total of 6,416 Series 72 Roadsters, although the specific number of Sport Roadsters included in that figure is not known.

An ad in a 1928 issue of *Automobile Trade Journal* premiered the new Sport Roadster along with the Series 72 Town Sedan:

Two new body models, a sport roadster with rumble seat and a town sedan, are announced by the Chrysler Sales Corp. as additions to its "72" line. The roadster lists for $1,595 and the town sedan for $1,695, both f.o.b. Detroit. The roadster

The DeSoto was priced to compete with Dodge, and its announcement in April 1928 was a deliberate attempt to unnerve the firm of Dillon, Read, & Company, which at the time owned Dodge Brothers. It worked. A month later they sold Dodge to Chrysler.

Walter Chrysler, left, and the "Three Musketeers," Carl Breer, Fred Zeder, and Owen Skelton, with a brand new 1928 Chrysler.

The 1926 Chrysler two-door roadster, moderately priced at $1,625, included a rumble seat and the popular golf club door.

is conspicuous for its striking color combination. The top is a light tan and the body a rich Thorn brown. Striping is of gold bronze and a bright orange appears on the narrow streamline panels across and several inches beyond the doors. Moorish brown is used on fenders, splash guards, hood sills, radiator, etc., while standard wood wheels are of the same color trimmed with Thorn brown. The car has a folding type windshield with nickeled stanchions, drum-type nickel-plated headlamps, nickel-plated tail lamps and side lamps. A generous size golf compartment is built into one side of the body.

The "72" line also consisted of six other models: Roadster, Two-Passenger Coupe, Four-Passenger Coupe, Close-Coupled Sedan, Royal Sedan, and Crown Sedan.

The interior of all Series 72 models was new as well, with Chrysler stylists changing from an oval instrument panel design to one with an oblong fascia. The steering wheel rim was made thinner and both the throttle and headlight controls were placed around the center of the steering wheel hub so that the driver did not need to remove his hands from the wheel in order to switch on the headlights.

At the upper end of the market, the Imperial line continued to expand with a new Imperial Town Car added in 1927, and in 1928 an all-new 136-inch-wheel-base chassis carrying an even more powerful 309-cubic-inch six-cylinder engine rated at 100 horsepower.

During the latter half of the 1920s, Chrysler made quite a name for itself in Europe. In 1928, the Sport Roadster was one fast automobile, and Chrysler entered a team of four roadsters, two Series "72" and two Imperials, in the Grand Prix at LeMans. The team placed third and fourth in its class, with the winning car averaging 64.5 miles per hour for the run. The cars went on to the Belgium 24-hour race, where the Imperial took second place, and the Series "72" Red Heads finished a respectable third and sixth. In 1929 a new Series 65 Roadster set an unparalleled record at the famed German Avus Ring by clocking 53,170 miles in four straight weeks of nonstop driving. The only breaks were for gas, tires, and to change drivers. Renowned French race driver Louis Chiron was so impressed with the accomplishment that he not only endorsed Chrysler products in France, but purchased a Chrysler to use as his personal car. From this time on, the cars from Highland Park, Michigan, would be among the most highly regarded in France, as well as throughout much of Europe.

THE MERGER THAT GUARANTEED THE FUTURE

If Walter Chrysler had learned one thing from Billy Durant, it was the power of diversification. While Chrysler believed that Durant had gone too far in his quest to "own everything," he knew that the road to success meant competing in more than one or two price ranges. Like GM and Ford, Chrysler Corporation would have to offer a wide variety of models to be competitive.

In one year Chrysler put himself in a league with Ford and GM by announcing Plymouth as a low-price leader (essentially replacing the lowest-priced Model 52 Chryslers for the 1929 model year). For added measure, DeSoto was created to compete with rival models from independent automaker Dodge, founded by brothers John and Horace. Former Henry Ford cronies and brilliant engineers, the Dodge brothers went into business for themselves in 1914 after their stock holdings in Ford Motor Company made them multimillionaires. (In 1917 Henry Ford was pressured into paying the Dodge Brothers $25 million for their 10 percent stake in Ford Motor Company!)

DeSoto had been created, in part, to calculatedly unnerve the New York banking firm of Dillon, Read, & Company, which at the time held the title to Dodge Brothers. Following the death of both John and Horace in 1920 (they both caught the flu at the National Automobile Show in January and never recovered), it had been a slow downhill ride for Dodge. In 1925 John and Horace's widows had sold Dodge to Dillon, Read & Company for $146 million, making them two of the

This custom-bodied 1927 Imperial 80 five-seat Town Sedan was built for Walter Chrysler's wife, Della, pictured with the car.

In 1928 Walter Chrysler purchased Dodge. The sale was billed as "the largest consolidation in the history of the automobile industry." Chrysler simply said, "It was one of the soundest acts of my life." Pictured is a 1929 Dodge DA four-door sedan.

wealthiest women in America. John's widow, Matilda, married lumber broker Alfred G. Wilson, and financed the construction of Meadow Brook Hall in Rochester, Michigan, which was completed in 1929. Often called an American castle, the Hall (now part of Oakland University, which was founded by Matilda Dodge Wilson) exemplified the lavish lifestyles of wealthy twentieth century American industrialists.

In 1928 this statement did not necessarily apply to Clarence Dillon and his associates, who were easily unnerved by any changes in the automotive industry. The announcement by Chrysler Corporation of the competitively priced DeSoto line that April was a change they were just not prepared to deal with. Walter Chrysler

had applied just the right amount of pressure and achieved the desired result. Clarence Dillon phoned.

After a marathon bargaining session in May between Dillon and Walter P. Chrysler, who had sequestered the investment banker in a suite at the New York Ritz-Carlton for three days and nights of almost nonstop negotiations, Chrysler emerged as the new owner of Dodge. *Automobile Trade Journal* noted that the sale of Dodge Brothers to Chrysler was "the largest consolidation in the history of the automobile industry." Chrysler simply said, "It was one of the soundest acts of my life."

While this merger would ultimately spell the demise of DeSoto in the 1950s, in 1928 it gave Chrysler Corporation three competitively-priced model lines to

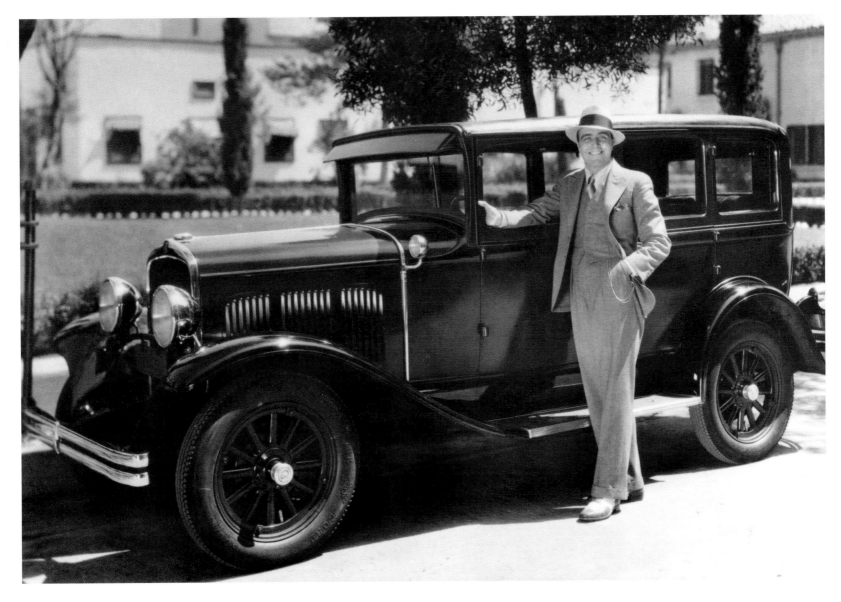

complement its luxurious Chrysler and Imperial series, and with the acquisition of Dodge, the Chrysler sales network was expanded to more than 8,000 dealerships. Two years later it would also give Chrysler an edge over rival independents and a diversity of product and pricing shared only with Ford and General Motors.

As the 1920s roared to an end in 1929, Chrysler completed its first five full years of production in 11th place among American automakers, a far more enviable position than one might think. With Dodge, Plymouth, and DeSoto as individual lines, the combined Chrysler Corporation had delivered over 375,000 cars for the 1929 model year, and the Chrysler brand alone had outpaced both Packard and Cadillac. There were now

Chrysler assembly plants operating in Canada, in Great Britain, and in Antwerp, Belgium. Chrysler Corporation was gunning for the "Big Two" and had GM and Ford square in its sights when the bears came charging down Wall Street in October of 1929.

Though the stock market crash humbled the nation by the end of 1929, no one, not even Walter P. Chrysler, could foresee the long-term consequences. A new decade was about to dawn, and the future still looked promising. For Chrysler, more so than any other American automaker, it would be. The company Walter Chrysler had built from the rubble of Maxwell-Chalmers closed out the decade as one of the most successful automakers in Detroit.

Comparably priced with the Dodge was Chrysler Corporation's DeSoto line. Initially created to compete with Dodge, before Chrysler purchased the company in 1928, the stately DeSoto Model K sedan sold for $995.

CHAPTER 3

WALTER P. CHRYSLER AND THE GREAT DEPRESSION

Facing the worst of times

America was in financial shock, new car sales plunged to an all-time low, and nowhere could the sound of belts tightening be heard louder than in Detroit. Wall Street's tumble from the storied heights of the late 1920s was more than a market correction, as many analysts and industry pundits had predicted. For many it was the beginning of the end.

Despite a stumbling economy, which had fallen flat on its face by 1930, Chrysler Corporation was one of the most profitable automakers in the nation, offering a wide variety of models, the latest advances in engineering and body design, and most of all at a price competitive with cars from Cadillac, Chevrolet, Buick, Ford, Lincoln, and Packard. The problem was,

Among the most desirable of the 1932 Imperials was the sporty Convertible Sedan like this one from the Frank Kleptz collection. With the Robert's full-length hood the car looked a mile long.

LeBaron bodies were all-steel construction (no wood framing), which was substantially stronger, even in an open car like the CG roadster. Chrysler marketing underscored the strength of all-steel construction with an outrageous publicity stunt. They took a four-door Imperial sedan to Coney Island and arranged for an elephant to stand atop a platform placed on the car's roof. Both elephant and Imperial came away unscathed.

that despite competitive pricing, fewer and fewer people were opening their pocketbooks. A great deal wasn't that great if you were worried that you might be out of work by the end of the year.

Chrysler eased into 1930 with mostly carryover models for the first few months and then began offering the new models in the spring. During the production hiatus, Chrysler had realigned its products in anticipation of diminishing sales, eliminating the Dodge-built six and replacing it with a Chrysler-built engine. There were five different versions in use throughout the entire Chrysler Corporation product line, including a new, lower-priced 195.6-cubic-inch six for the entry-level 1930 Chrysler CJ series.

With Cadillac having stunned the automotive world with the introduction of both V-12 and V-16 engines to go with its already successful line of eights, Chrysler's mostly six-cylinder line of cars was beginning

to lose some of its allure among those who could still contemplate the thought of purchasing a new car. Chrysler would not be far behind for long.

In 1927 Fred Zeder had started development of a new Chrysler straight eight, and Depression be damned, it was ready for 1930. The decision that stunned some observers was Walter Chrysler's announcement that the new engine would not be available for the 1930 Imperial. Instead the two new straight eights were only offered in Dodge and DeSoto models.

This proved a wise choice, as the Dodge and DeSoto models were more affordable and the eight-cylinder engines made them immediately desirable. The Imperial also required a larger engine than either of the new eights, 207.7 cubic inches for the DeSotos and 220.7 cubic inches for the Dodge. The Imperials would have to go another year with the big six under their hoods while Zeder and his staff completed a larger displacement eight for the big Chryslers. Those who could afford an Imperial in 1931 discovered that it had been well worth the wait.

SURVIVAL OF THE MOST DIVERSIFIED

During the Depression, many of the automotive industry's most revered marques were almost idled as sales plummeted and unemployment lines grew longer, yet Chrysler continued to introduce new models almost every year, and at the same time make

impressive advancements in both engineering and technology. Even in the face of Cadillac's 12- and 16-cylinder models, Chrysler appeared undaunted. As Walter P. Chrysler explained in his autobiography, "We had to cut salaries, reduce operations, retrench in every way. But no matter how gloomy the outlook, I never cut a single penny from the budget of our research department."

It was Chrysler's dogged ambition to continually advance design and technology that kept the company on the cutting edge, while most of the competition was cutting back.

The Imperial CG models were built on a new 145-inch wheelbase, the longest yet for any Chrysler model. The LeBaron bodies, like this handsome roadster, were designed by Ralph Roberts and Carl W. Van Ranst, who had been hired by Chrysler as a consultant. Van Ranst had previously worked for E. L. Cord on the L-29.

The Chrysler division alone offered eight different series containing a total of 52 distinct body styles in 1931. In addition to the Series CJ, Series 66, Series 70, and "New Series" CM six-cylinder models, Chrysler introduced a line-up of four new eight-cylinder engines, the first straight eights in the company's history, the largest of which powered the new 1931 Imperial CG line.

The most dramatic LeBaron body styles for the CG chassis were the roadster and dual cowl phaeton, the latter being one of the most elegant designs of the Classic Era. Originally designed for Duesenberg by Ray Dietrich, the dual cowl phaeton was also the body style of choice for LeBaron-bodied Packards. The Chrysler CG versions were designed by Ralph Roberts and his assistant, Roland Stickney, whom Roberts described as "the finest sketch artist in the history of automotive design."

For the new 1931 Imperials, like this one from the John McMullen collection, Chrysler stylists copied the radiator and hood scallops used by European automaker Vauxhall, however, without obtaining Vauxhall's permission. Chrysler also restyled the Imperial grille to resemble the popular Cord L-29. Somehow these disparate elements looked better on the Imperial than on the original vehicles from which Boss Chrysler's designers found their "influence".
John McMullen Collection

Roberts, like many designers in the 1930s, could not draw and had to rely on a sketch artist to interpret his ideas and put them down on paper. Roberts had learned automotive design from the very best, Ray Dietrich, Tom Hibbard, and Howard "Dutch" Darrin, who was also disinclined to put pencil to paper.

The Imperials featured a striking vee'd radiator shell similar to some of Harry Miller's racing cars, and not too different in appearance from that of the popular Cord L-29. This was no coincidence. A little outright thievery in the name of marketing was not beyond the Chrysler design and engineering staff. For that matter, it was pretty much common practice throughout the automotive industry. Legendary stylist Alex Tremulis, who would later design the 1941 Chrysler Thunderbolt concept car, once said that it wasn't thievery, " . . . it was merely one designer *influencing* another." (Tremulis was later involved in litigation over the 1950 Studebaker front end design and its similarity to the Tucker Torpedo, which he had designed for Preston Tucker in 1946.)

The Imperial CG roadsters, and dual cowl phaetons in particular, were well suited to the sense of presence the large radiator shell vested in them. Behind the long length of hood and low cowl line, LeBaron braced the windshield glass in a slanting vee'd frame following the motif established by the Imperial's grille design. One unusual feature of the LeBaron-bodied roadsters and phaetons was that the windshield wiper mechanisms were actually drilled through the windshield glass.

The spirited performance from the Imperial's 385-cubic-inch, 125-horsepower straight eight was impressive considering the sheer size of the cars, which were built on a new 145-inch-wheelbase chassis, the largest Chrysler had produced up to that time. With the greatest swept volume of the new eights, the Imperial CG engine had its own version of the L-head design with a bore and stroke of 3 1/2x5 inches, and a compression ratio of 5.2:1, developing sufficient torque and horsepower to deliver the massive phaetons and roadsters from a stand to 60 miles per hour in just 20 seconds, and to a top speed of 100 miles per hour. To prove the power of the CG engine, in 1932 a Chrysler dealer in Ohio drove an Imperial roadster a distance of 100 miles in just 62 minutes.

A special feature of the new Chrysler eight-cylinder models was a unique dual range transmission with four forward speeds. Chrysler suggested that the first gear, indicated as low-low (with a 12.9:1 ratio) and set aside to the far left of the "H" pattern, be used only in

The dual-cowl phaeton design was a staple of the entire Chrysler line. This handsome 1930 Model 77 was a lower-priced alternative to the Imperial, and no less attractive a car.

emergency situations, such as on steep grades, or if bogged down in mud or snow. For normal starts, second gear, at 8.98:1, was recommended, with third, a 5.39:1 ratio, being used for acceleration and passing at highway speeds. This was really the performance ratio for propelling the roadster from 50 to 70 miles per hour. Top gear, with a 3.82:1 ratio, was for quiet, economical cruising, or reaching that lofty century mark. To gain better fuel economy, the CG was also equipped with an overdrive, engaged at speeds above 40–45 miles per hour by lifting off the accelerator pedal, waiting for the OD to kick in with a click, and then quickly depressing the throttle once again. Maximum speeds in the top three gears of approximately 43, 73, and 100 miles per hour were achieved with the four-speed in track tests, making the Imperial faster than either the Cadillac or Lincoln eight-cylinder models.

The Imperials used "biflex" bumpers, which were both stylish and functional. Biflex was the trade name

of the highest quality bumper one could purchase. It was made of a loaded spring steel. On impact they would compress and reflex back to shape—the 1930s version of today's low impact bumpers.

LeBaron interiors were luxurious but not overly ornate. Roberts endowed the Imperials with a sense of elegance more than ostentation. LeBarons were luxuriously upholstered in supple leathers, including the side panels, door caps, and padded dashboard, an idea Roberts borrowed from Dutch Darrin. The instruments were all white with black numerals, and simply arranged across the center of the dash panel.

Purchased by celebrities and a roster of dignitaries including New York Mayor Al Smith and race driver Billy Arnold, only 100 roadsters and 85 dual cowl phaetons were produced for the 1931 model year, making them among the rarest of all Chrysler Imperial models.

Though outside influences should have dictated otherwise, in 1931 Chrysler built one of the industry's first advanced design and engineering studios, which was headed by Carl Breer, Fred Zeder, and Owen Skelton. The trio had euphemistically come to be known around Detroit as Chrysler's Three Musketeers. Indeed, they were the triumvirate behind Walter P. Chrysler, and the

Left and above:
This 1932 Imperial convertible sedan from the Nethercutt Collection shows the impressive size of this car, which was nearly 20 feet in length and easily one of the most attractive motorcars of the era. The price as shown was $3,595. A comparable V-8 Cadillac model had a list of $3,495.

Walter P. Chrysler's 1932 Imperial Speedster was a one-of-a-kind design built on the short 135-inch CH wheelbase instead of the Imperial Custom's 146-inch platform, which made the lengthy Imperial hood appear even longer. After a complete restoration in 1990 by current owner Sam Mann, the car went on to win Best of Show at the 1991 Pebble Beach Concours d'Elegance.

men most responsible for the company's innovative and highly successful ideas throughout the 1920s and 1930s.

While the Imperials gained eights in 1931, the DeSoto eight was discontinued and the line was offered with flat-head six-cylinder engines, making the 1930 models pretty rare cars today. Dodge kept the straight eight under its hood until 1933, after which a progression of sixes were offered for Plymouth, Dodge, and DeSoto models, leaving Chrysler and Imperial models as the only eight-cylinder cars.

DIVIDE TO CONQUER

In 1932 Chrysler divided the Imperial line into two distinct categories, semicustoms, designated as the CH series and built on a new 135-inch wheelbase; and the senior CL series, also known as Imperial Custom, assembled on a new chassis with a 146-inch stretch between the axles. Imperial models consisted of roadster, coupe, phaeton, convertible sedan, five- and seven-passenger sedans, and seven-passenger limousine.

The most distinctive Imperials were the long hood CL models, designed by Ralph Roberts and built to order by LeBaron in eight different body styles. The full length hood, which extended over the cowl to the base of the windshield, gave the Imperials the long, lean look of competitive 12-cylinder models from Lincoln, Packard, and Cadillac. Combined with the new vee'd radiator and grille shell, the Imperial had one of the most imposing front end designs of the era, and in the opinion of many modern-day collectors, the 1932 Chrysler LeBaron CL Imperials were the best-styled cars the company ever built.

Within the Imperial line the most popular open car was the convertible sedan offered in both CH and CL series, with a base price of $2,195 on the short wheelbase CH chassis, and $3,595 for the CL. The most expensive semicustoms in 1932, a total of only 152 CH convertible sedans were produced, along with a mere 49 Custom Imperial versions.

"LeBarons were always limited in number," recalled company president and chief designer Ralph

The close-coupled body design gave the Imperial a stately appearance. This model was popular among the well-to-do, who preferred the Chrysler to more ostentatious marques like Packard during the Depression.

Roberts in a 1981 interview with the author. "The stock market crash reduced the number of customers willing to pay the price of a custom-built body, but LeBaron was far better off than most, supplying semicustom bodies for Chrysler, Packard, and Lincoln from the Briggs facility in Detroit."

Back in 1928 Roberts had sold controlling interest in LeBaron to the Briggs Body Company, moving the firm's principal manufacturing from New York to Detroit. "These cars were distinguished by the *LeBaron Detroit* nameplate," noted Roberts.

Despite a declining market for high-priced luxury cars, Chrysler did better than most in the early 1930s. The CL series cars were built to order, and with all body styles combined, only 220 were delivered in 1932. Total Chrysler production for the year, which included 47 different styles and 8 distinct series, amounted to 25,291 cars. DeSoto came in slightly lower for the year with 24,496 cars sold, and Dodge beat them both together

The front compartment of the CL Imperial was lavishly trimmed in woods and the instruments were framed in a beautiful polished metal fascia.

with 50,100 deliveries. That would have made a pretty decent year for Chrysler Corporation, but Plymouth's new models skyrocketed in 1932 with a total of 180,006 sales!

As the Depression wore on, more Chryslers were finding their way into the hands of affluent owners than competitive makes from Cadillac and Packard. At the worst possible time for the Detroit establishment, Chrysler had truly become a force to be reckoned with. Despite having to cut production in 1932, Chrysler sold more luxury cars than Oldsmobile, Cadillac-LaSalle, or Packard, and to a great extent the Imperial's success was the result of Robert's handsome long hood concept.

The low point of the Depression came and went in 1933 and Chrysler managed to increase sales by a small

EDSEL HATED IT, WALTER LOVED IT

AN INTERVIEW WITH LEBARON'S RALPH ROBERTS

Chrysler's striking long hood design, says LeBaron's Ralph Roberts, was a pure twist of fate. "I saw the original long style hood on a trip to Paris in 1931. No one had done this in America, so I decided to try it. I had one built on a Lincoln chassis to show Edsel Ford. We had become good friends over the years, and he used to come over to LeBaron, sit down at a drafting table and suggest ideas, or just chit-chat about cars in general. I think he was a designer at heart, and he usually had very good instincts. But as it turned out, Edsel didn't like the long hood design. Hated it in fact. 'It's awful. It's a terrible looking thing,' he said. 'The front end looks like a coffin.' Well, that was pretty much the end of it, I thought."

Roberts had the prototype rolled out into the parking lot so it would be away from Walter P. Chrysler and a handful of board members who were coming over to look at some proposals for new models. "Well, when they arrived someone saw the Lincoln and pointed it out to Walter. He took one look and said, 'My God, what's that?' I said it was just a design we were experimenting with. Chrysler was beaming, 'Can't we have that? That long, long hood is really something!' I said, 'Sure, you can have it.'"

Edsel Ford's loss was Walter Chrysler's gain.

The long hood design, however, didn't remain a Chrysler exclusive for long. Alexis de Sakhnoffsky's famed false hood design, used on 1933 Packards, was essentially the same idea, and by the mid-1930s, running the back edge of the hood panels over the cowl and up to the base of the windshield had almost become *de rigueur* on custom bodies, as had many LeBaron styling traits.

"We had a lot of big accounts in the 1920s, but the trouble was, once we designed a car we were through with it. We finally reached a point where our designs were being used to make more than one car, while we were only getting paid one time. Ray and I decided to expand, and in 1923 we merged with the Bridgeport Body Company. Now we could produce the bodies that we designed. LeBaron, Inc., went from a staff of only 3, to over 40 craftsmen at Bridgeport, and we gained a second design studio."

LeBaron's future would ultimately end up in Robert's hands. In 1923 founding partner Thomas Hibbard left to form Hibbard & Darrin of Paris, with his friend Howard "Dutch" Darrin, and in 1926, Ray Dietrich moved to Detroit to start his own design firm. Roberts merged LeBaron, Inc., with Briggs shortly after, establishing LeBaron Detroit, which became one of Chrysler's principal suppliers throughout the 1930s and 1940s.

"We built some really nice cars back then," Roberts said in a 1986 interview. "It is kind of odd to look back on the classic era now, because at the time we were building these cars, we never considered them anything special. History has made them very glamorous. Made them art objects. The custom body builders didn't have anything like that in mind. Coachbuilding was never a fine art, but it was an applied art, a commercial art. We enjoyed our work, even found it exciting at times, as the design of our products advanced in quantum leaps. You might look back on the 1920s and 1930s as the Golden Age of the automobile, with the custom coachbuilders of the era, to use a trite expression, the right guys, for the right thing, at the right time."

At Briggs and LeBaron, the timing was always right, and in December 1953, Chrysler purchased Briggs, thus assuring its designs and proprietary ownership of the LeBaron name, which has been used by Chrysler Corporation for more than a half-century.

margin to 32,220 cars. The year also marked the second time that a Chrysler Imperial had been chosen by the Indianapolis 500 stewards to serve as the pacesetter for the Memorial Day classic. A Chrysler Imperial four-passenger roadster was first chosen in 1926, and for 1933 it was an Imperial Custom Eight convertible roadster with a semicustom body by LeBaron. A very rare car, only nine Indy Pace Car replicas were built, with a price starting at $3,295. With luxury car sales tumbling, Chrysler was able to make up the loss with a sweeping increase in the low-priced field that had once been dominated by Ford and Chevrolet. Plymouth was the best selling product Chrysler Corporation had, competitively priced with Ford and Chevrolet models and equipped with features that neither crosstown rival could offer, such as all-steel construction, and four-wheel hydraulic brakes.

While most companies were trying to keep their heads above water in the early 1930s, Chrysler was swimming laps in the Detroit motor pool. With Plymouth as the entry level leader (having risen to the number three seller in the nation in 1932), DeSoto, Dodge, and the full line of Chrysler and Imperial models gave Chrysler Corporation a car in virtually every price class, from under $500 for a Plymouth sedan, to $3,400 for a semicustom Imperial.

THE CHRYSLER AIRFLOW: LIKE A REED IN THE WIND

Chrysler's propensity for pushing the accepted limits of contemporary styling (a preoccupation in which, fortunately, the company still indulges) reached further into the future than any other American automaker in

The Red Head engine gave the Imperial the highest possible performance in its class. In 1933 output was rated at 135 horsepower.

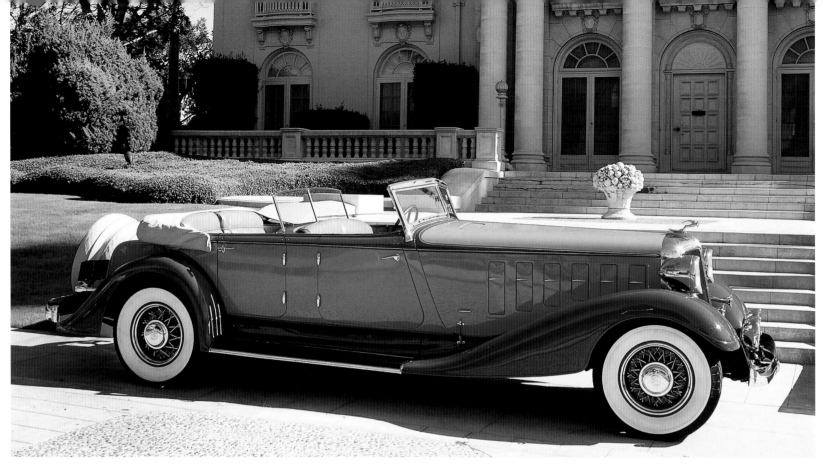

Ralph Roberts designed this one-off LeBaron CL Sport Phaeton to suit his particular taste, which was a bit different from the other examples bodied for Chrysler in 1933. "There were a number of unusual or experimental ideas tried on my car," said Roberts. "One was an extended fender line at the rear with twin spares, instead of the usual sidemount spares. It made the car so long that it wouldn't fit in our freight elevator at the Detroit factory. They had to remove the rear tire mount just to get it out of the building!" The car was literally built from the last remaining parts in the LeBaron factory, since work was already under way for the 1934 LeBaron Airflows.

THE BOSS'S CAR

The call came from the man whose name was on the building. Walter P. Chrysler wanted the experimental Custom Body Shop in Highland Park to build a one-off speedster to his specifications. Ordering the custom Imperial was Walter's subtle way of getting the guys in engineering to stretch their imaginations and go one step beyond the current technology. He gave them a list of goals: increase the power, make the car easier to operate, and give it head turning style. The boys in Highland Park didn't let him down.

In designing the Speedster, the staff had to literally perfect features few automakers had even considered in the early 1930s, including an automatic choke and a gas pedal–actuated starter with a unique (to Chrysler) automatic stall restart mechanism. The Chrysler 384.8-cubic-inch straight eight was equipped with an experimental aluminum high-compression head that boosted output from 125 horsepower to a rousing 160 horsepower, and an experimental clutch with a pendulum-activated valve that automatically disengaged the transmission in a panic stop, thus preventing the engine from stalling. About the only standard item on the car was the three-speed transmission, and even that was coupled to a special high-speed rear end.

Although "The Boss" favored Ralph Roberts' lengthy CL hood, Chrysler had his Speedster built on the shorter 135-inch CH wheelbase chassis, which made the LeBaron hoodline look a mile long. The body design for the Speedster followed other LeBaron styling cues as well, although it was not a LeBaron. The lines were penned by Herbert Weissinger, Chrysler's leading stylist.

The basic design had actually appeared two years earlier as a rendering in a 1930 edition of *Fortune* magazine covering Walter Chrysler and his company. Among various drawings depicting future Chrysler designs was one showing a custom roadster with pontoon fenders, a short, rakish windshield, and no running boards.

The Imperial Speedster's present owner, noted car collector Sam Mann, says that the Chrysler Speedster was likely inspired by European styling trends. According to Mann, "This car and the rendering in *Fortune* bear extensive French influence, most specifically that of Letourneur et Marchand, and perhaps to a lesser extent, Fernandez et Darrin."

Built on Chrysler's new reinforced double-drop boxed frame, the Speedster's lines were strikingly low, giving the car an image of uncommon grace and speed. Virtually handmade, the body panels were all aluminum, and the handsome pontoon-style fenders formed from sheet steel. Special features designed for Chrysler included step plates instead of running boards— a design first seen on French coachwork in the late 1920s—a fully concealed folding top, a racy, sweptback, cut-down windshield, quad horns, and locking storage compartments in both front fenders.

The exterior color scheme was also custom, a unique blend of browns and reds, which Chrysler stylists called Prescott brown. In contrast to the dark exterior, the interior was a study in "How many shades of bright red can you combine in one car?" The upholstery and interior trim were red leather. The steering wheel, carpeting and floor mats, brake, clutch, and gas pedal were red, and even the AM radio, a feature rarely found in the early 1930s, was red.

The Speedster became a promotional vehicle for Chrysler Corporation, and was used to advertise Chrysler products at various dealerships around the country. Its most prominent appearance may have been in illustration form in a 1930s Kendall Oil advertisement.

Walter Chrysler gave the car to his son, Walter Jr., and it remained at his estate in Provincetown, Massachusetts, until the 1960s. Not long after he became the third owner in November 1989, Sam Mann put the one-of-a-kind Speedster in the able hands of his restoration crew. One year later, it emerged exactly as it had looked when it rolled out of Chrysler's Custom Body Shop in 1932.

The Imperial Speedster was a rolling test bed for Chrysler engineering, and says Mann about driving this incredible car, "It's almost like a modern automobile. It accelerates with the speed of a V-12 and cruises silently and effortlessly at 70 miles per hour. It is really quite spectacular. Everything one would have expected of a car built for 'The Boss.' "

In 1934 Chrysler headed off in a new direction with the streamlined Airflow. The first cars were strikingly radical in their appearance, and they left some people at a loss for words. The words were, "I'll take one." The overwhelming waterfall grille, which characterized the aerodynamic sweep of the front end, was too much for most people, and in 1935 it was redesigned. Today it is considered a work of art.

1934. In this one instance, though, Chrysler may have reached a bit too far.

The Airflow was unlike anything American car buyers had seen. Its shape was dictated almost entirely by the principles of aircraft aerodynamics, and while Chrysler's radical approach sent the world of automotive design reeling in 1934, it did not have the same effect on new car buyers.

Carl Breer had been inspired by aircraft design for years, and when the Airflow project began in 1932, he even consulted with aviation pioneer Orville Wright. The Airflow shape, even Chrysler's choice of the Airflow name, stringently adhered to the aerodynamic principles evolving throughout the early 1930s, both in the fields of aviation and automobile design. No one, however, with the exception of conceptualist stylist John Tjaarda, took as radical an approach in the 1930s as Carl Breer.

First, scale models were tested in a wind tunnel built in Highland Park; then a series of full-size models were used to refine the car's shape until it was as efficient as the technology of the day allowed. A running prototype called the "Trifon Special" was built in the latter part of 1932. The teardrop shape gave the car a sweptback look accentuated by a short, curved nose with faired-in headlights—the very features that would be seen on the 1934 Airflow. Walter Chrysler liked it, Zeder, Skelton, and Breer liked it, and that was enough in those halcyon days to get a car into production. What no one seemed to ask, or even take into consideration, was whether the public would like it.

Styling aside, the Airflow was an engineering masterpiece. It utilized a beam-and-truss body, an early interpretation of unibody construction, blending body and chassis

The DeSoto was popular enough in 1935 that the chief steward of the 23rd Indianapolis 500-Mile Race chose an Airflow over a Ford V-8, which was the Official Pace Car for the Memorial Day classic.

Although the Airflow was beginning to sell a little better, DeSoto bid farewell to the aerodynamic look in 1937 and doubled its sales to 81,775 cars. Shown is the 1937 S-3 convertible coupe.

together to provide added strength without increasing overall weight. The Airflow's interior was expansive—the rear seat measured 50 inches across. Driver and passengers literally sat within the perimeter of the car's wheelbase, since the engine extended beyond the front axle, thus allowing more available interior space. This unusual arrangement (in 1934), could be considered the forerunner of the now popular Chrysler cab-forward design.

By 1935 all Chrysler Imperials carried the same rounded, aerodynamic styling penned by Chrysler stylist Oliver Clark and later refined by Norman Bel Geddes. The design carried over into the entire DeSoto line as well, and while the streamlined Airflow shape was very functional, it was neither as elegant nor as well proportioned as everyone originally thought. The Airflow was a bit much for the average American consumer to swallow, especially when there were so many manufacturers trying to sell conventional looking cars at bargain prices.

The Chrysler version of the Airflow was offered on four different wheelbases, and in body styles ranging from a business coupe to the luxurious $5,000 Custom

continued on page 56

THE MAJOR BOWES IMPERIAL AIRFLOW LIMOUSINE

"The sweetest chariot in the land is a big, purring, glistening, superdeluxe Chrysler Imperial owned by the famous amateur's impresario, Maj. Edward Bowes." So wrote *Look* magazine in its June 18, 1940, issue. The story went on to tell a tale about Walter Chrysler personally designing the car for his friend Maj. Bowes. That Walter P. actually put pen to paper and drafted the custom LeBaron body is highly doubtful, but he most certainly issued the order to make this the most luxurious Airflow limousine ever built. Some $25,000 later it was that, and more.

The Airflow CW received the full LeBaron treatment. More than just an automobile, Bowes needed an office on wheels, since he traveled to a different city each week to broadcast the *Amateur Hour*. The dark green and gold Airflow limousine was a combination home, office, and restaurant on wheels for the radio celebrity. At 20 feet in length, 74 inches in height, and fitted with a custom interior closer to that of a private rail car, the 7,000-pound Bowes CW lumbered along America's highways and byways from 1937 to 1941.

After the car was completed in March of 1937, Chrysler Corporation, which sponsored the *Bowes Amateur Hour*, issued a news release stating that the custom LeBaron Airflow had ". . . all the comforts of home, all the convenience of the best-appointed office and all the luxury of a maharajah's palace. This is beyond doubt the world's most extraordinary automobile in the variety and magnificence of its fittings."

Ingeniously fitted into the rear compartment were all sorts of devices for serving food and beverages, a foldout writing desk, an electric razor, a vanity with comb and brush, and storage drawers for wardrobe changes. Two swiveling jump seats were built in to accommodate Major Bowes' personal secretary and an assistant for on-the-road conferences.

The Airflow's novel interior was designed by F. A. Selje, Chrysler's chief interior body designer. The custom coachwork was done by LeBaron Detroit with chief body engineer John Votypka in direct charge. Noted Chrysler, "It is the most elaborate job of refitting an interior of a car ever attempted, and it has worked out to the complete satisfaction of the fastidious Major Bowes."

The exterior of the car was painted Brewster green and the interior upholstery was done in two shades of green Laidlaw broadcloth named "Major Bowes light" and "Major Bowes dark" in honor of the owner. The front compartment was upholstered in two shades of green leather, and all of the interior trim in the rear compartment was done in Dirigold, a nontarnishable metal resembling gold. The complementary color scheme was chosen by Mr. Selje because the colors were "appropriate for the early autumn of life," and suited Major Bowes station.

There were many fine details designed into the car's interior, such as a Venetian blind in the rear window, hand-carved jade inlays in the door panels depicting the muses of the radio, and an electrically operated divider window. The inside of the ventilating portion of the rear quarter windows was finished with amber colored mirrors, and on the outside they were painted to match the body, thus providing the major with a little added privacy.

The greatest ingenuity was used in designing the console that was placed on the division between the front and rear compartments. At the top center of this console was an instrument grouping that included thermometer, clock, and compass. Above these, two humidors, a cigar lighter and ash tray, all of which were finished with ornamental metal covers. On each side of the instrument grouping were compartments for bottles and glasses, and directly below that, a foldout serving table. In the bottom of the console was a serving compartment with a stainless steel drawer containing a thermal storage bin for ice and cold beverages, and on the other side, cold storage for fruit and sandwiches. Even today's modern limousines lack most of these features!

The 1937 CW owned by radio star Major Edward Bowes was used extensively between 1937 and 1941 when Bowes broadcasted his national radio show from a different city each week. In 1937 the Bowes Amateur Hour was live from the Indiana Theater in Terre Haute, Indiana. The car, owned today by collector Frank Kleptz of Terre Haute, is posed in front of the restored Indiana Theater, just as it was in 1937.

Ensconced in the rear compartment of his 1937 Imperial Airflow limousine, Major Edward Bowes had all the comforts of home at his disposal. LeBaron had designed the custom CW to Bowes' exact needs, which included dining, wardrobe, and desk for work. Built at a cost of $25,000, it was the most expensive Airflow produced. Frank Kleptz collection

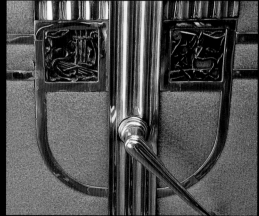

The ornate decorations in the rear compartment included hand-carved jade representations of the "muses of the radio."

For the long drives between cities, and from his home in Ossining to New York City, the 50-inch-wide rear seat in the Major Bowes car was designed like a sitting room divan, with plush, down-filled cushions and a seatback padded to the shoulder line. The seat was divided by a luxuriously upholstered folding center armrest, behind which a fold-down desk and a compartment to store both a thermos bottle and toiletries could be found. The right-hand arm rest contained the rear compartment radio controls, an ash receiver, and buttons for operating the division window. The left armrest had a second humidor and ash receiver. For an added touch of elegance, all of the hardware in the rear compartment, including the brackets on the jump seats, were finished in Dirigold.

The interior of the Major Bowes Airflow limousine was done in green. Two-tone leather was used for the chauffeur's compartment, and the rear was upholstered in two shades of green Laidlaw broadcloth named "Major Bowes light" and "Major Bowes dark" in honor of the owner.

The Airflow served Major Bowes up until the beginning of World War II. Chrysler records show that the car went back to them in 1941. It was then repainted black, equipped with a few additional features, and given to the U.S. Navy the following year; the Navy assigned it to Admiral Chester Nimitz as his personal staff car. It was used in Hawaii, and as the story goes, went with him to Guam, where it acquired nine bullet holes! No official explanation for this has ever been uncovered.

After the war it is believed that a newspaper correspondent purchased the car and had it shipped back to San Diego, California, where it was used by a limousine service. After that it all but vanished, as did radio as America's number one form of entertainment. A decade later people were glued to their B&W televisions and a likable ukelele-picking character named Arthur Godfrey was hosting a televised version of the *Amateur Hour*. As for the Major Bowes car, it fell into obscurity. Just another old Airflow parked and left to face the fate of so many others. (Oddly enough, for many old Airflows in the 1950s, that fate was to end up in Cuba, where many can still be found running to this day!)

In 1967 the Major Bowes car turned up in a graveyard of a used car lot in Pasadena, California, where collector Johnny McLean discovered the bullet riddled CW limousine. McLean purchased the car and began a restoration but passed away before it was completed. His widow sold the car to current owner Frank Kleptz of Terre Haute, Indiana, in 1979, and Frank completed the car's restoration over the next 3 1/2 years. Today, the CW is exactly as it was when it served as the radio talent scout's personal livery.

In 1937 Major Bowes broadcast the *Amateur Hour* from the regal Indiana Theater in Terre Haute. In 1999, the car returned to the very spot where it had been parked 62 years before, for a re-creation of Major Bowes visit in 1937. Thanks to the theater's owners and manager, the marquee was changed to read MAJOR BOWES, and an original theater one-sheet from the *Amateur Hour* was displayed. For one evening in 1999, it was 1937 all over again, and the Major Bowes Airflow was once more "The sweetest chariot in the land."

Continued from page 51

Imperial Airflow Series CW Limousine. (The lower-priced DeSoto Airflows were all six-cylinder cars built on a 115.5-inch wheelbase.) On Chrysler models the stretch between the wheels varied from the short 122.8-inch CU chassis, powered by a 299-cubic-inch L-head eight developing 122 horsepower; to the 128-inch-wheelbase CV eight, with a swept volume of 323.5 cubic inches and output of 130 horsepower; or the longer 137.5-inch CX version with 130 horsepower; and the mammoth 146-inch-wheelbase CW platform, driven by Chrysler's largest engine, a 384.84-cubic-inch straight eight delivering 145 horsepower.

From the beginning, a few of Chrysler's close associates had voiced concern over the Airflow, advising him to offer an alternative model line. One of those voices belonged to Chrysler's friend Ray Dietrich, who was now heading up the company's fledgling art and color department. Dietrich worked closely with the Briggs Manufacturing Company, which had become Chrysler's principal supplier of production and custom bodies, the latter through LeBaron Detroit, a Briggs subsidiary. The combined styling departments at Chrysler, Briggs, and LeBaron were second only in size to Harley Earl's art and color department at General Motors.

Dietrich saw to the reshaping of the Airflow design into the less radical Airstream, along with his old partner

Wow! In 1934 gasoline was just 10.5 cents a gallon, and the new DeSoto Airflow sold for only $995, regardless of body style.

Ralph Roberts at LeBaron, and one of Briggs' leading stylists, Phil Wright, who among other things had penned the innovative 1933 Pierce-Arrow Silver Arrow. Wright's design proposals were approved by Roberts, Dietrich, and Chrysler almost without change, and Briggs rushed a series of three body styles into production for 1935—sedan, coupe, and convertible.

Beneath the stylish coachwork, the Airstream utilized many Airflow designs, including the basic chassis layout and interior design. Offered in Chrysler and DeSoto versions, the Airstreams were available with inline six- and eight-cylinder engines with 93 and 110 horsepower. They also featured hydraulic brakes, Floating Power motor mounts, and all-synchromesh three-speed transmissions. The Airstreams helped Chrysler turn 1935 into the second best sales year up to that time, posting $35 million in profits—a windfall for stockholders, and to

Chrysler employees, who divided $2.3 million in bonuses. Such beneficence was all but unheard of in Depression-torn Detroit.

In the end, the Airflow could cut through the wind like a rapier, but it couldn't cut it on the showroom floor. Fortunately, Chrysler's lower-priced Airstream models, along with ever-increasing Plymouth sales (more than a half million in 1937 alone) allowed Chrysler Corporation to retain a respectable share of the new car market throughout the 1930s.

Although history has deemed it a failure, the Airflow did predict future styling, and by the late 1930s, the slightly updated Chrysler Airflows, which arrived in 1936, didn't appear all that unusual. Lincoln had the Tjaarda-inspired Zephyr, which was equally radical in appearance, and by 1941 the majority of automakers had let the wind help shape the future of American automobiles. But Chrysler had been the first.

The Airflow assembly line paint department circa 1934–1936.

CHRYSLER AT PEACE AND WAR

From building Airflows to Sherman tanks

In 1938 Chrysler finally laid the failed Airflow to rest after four frustrating years of trying to sell its futuristic concept to a buying public that simply didn't get it. Still, between 1934 and 1937, Chrysler's automotive technology had advanced further than in the period from 1924 to 1933, and there was little left to tie past and present together after the Airflow, save for the Chrysler engine and Imperial name. The classic era was beginning to wind down, and by 1939 the attrition rate among automakers was harrowing. Gone were many of the greatest and oldest automotive marques in America,

The 1939 Chrysler models like this Imperial Victoria Coupe had an unmistakably modern look about them—with contoured headlights built into the fenders, and a unique two-piece grille treatment that focused attention on the hoodline as never before.

Chrysler hit on a great idea in 1940 with the introduction of the Town & Country sedan wagon. The white ash and mahogany trim was actually part of the body structure, and the cars were literally rolling furniture. The bodies were manufactured by Pekin Wood Products in Helena, Arkansas, which became a subsidiary of Chrysler Corporation.

In 1940 Chrysler stylists at Briggs put pen to paper and designed two concept cars to be exhibited at auto shows around the country. Ralph Roberts of LeBaron (a subsidiary of Briggs) designed the sporty Newport dual-cowl phaeton, and former Cord stylist Alex Tremulis created the design for the futuristic Thunderbolt hardtop convertible.

including such legendary makes as Auburn, Cord, Duesenberg, Marmon, Franklin, and Pierce-Arrow. Chrysler, however, was well on the way to becoming one of Detroit's survivors, ending one of the greatest and most turbulent decades in American automotive history with the introduction of a totally redesigned series of cars.

While the Airflow had taken aerodynamic contouring to its most efficient profile, which, as history has proven was not the most attractive way to cheat the wind, aerodynamic styling had worked well for Cadillac with the 1933 Aero Dynamic Coupe, and would help Lincoln shape its future with the John Tjaarda, Briggs–designed Zephyr in 1936. In Europe, streamlined coachwork was all the rage, and the leading Parisian carrosserie—Figoni, Saoutchik, Franay, and Chapron—were designing cars so streamlined in appearance that they made the Airflow look like a 4x8 sheet of plywood. Ironically, they were not nearly as aerodynamic . . . just prettier.

In 1938 Chrysler equipped the Imperial line with a new 298.7-cubic-inch straight eight mounted atop a brand new double-drop X-girder frame equipped with a coil spring independent front suspension. Two wheelbase lengths were offered—125 inches for the standard Imperials, and 144 inches for Custom Imperials, which were powered by the large displacement 323.5-cubic-inch eight.

Custom coachwork was rarely seen by the 1940s, and only a handful of independent coachbuilders remained in business, among them the Derham Body Company in Rosemont, Pennsylvania, which built two of these extraordinary town cars in 1942.

Having sorted out its chassis and powertrain combinations, Chrysler turned its attention toward the post-Airflow era with all new coachwork for 1939, and the introduction of several innovative new features.

Topping the list was Chrysler's Cruise-and-Climb transmission, described in sales brochures as one of the most significant advancements in years:

The roadability of the new 1939 Chrysler cars astonishes everybody who experiences it. People say that the car seems to ride in a well-oiled groove . . . on curves and uneven roads, as well as on smooth highways.

Chrysler Corporation engineers sought and found a way to accomplish this seeming miracle, and the result of their inventive genius is embodied in today's Chrysler as the Cruise-and-Climb Transmission. It comes into operation whenever you want it at any car speed above 23 miles per hour, simply by lifting your foot momentarily from the accelerator pedal. And you can return to the conventional lower gear ratio whenever you need increased power or torque for fast acceleration or hill climbing, merely by pressing your accelerator to the floor board.

The 1939 sales brochure went on to explain the advantages of the new overdrive transmission with this rather interesting comparison:

If your engine turns over one-third fewer revolutions per mile, naturally it follows that your cylinders are filled with gas one-third fewer times. That means an appreciable saving in gasoline consumption. To put it another way, your Chrysler with

Cruise-and-Climb Transmission will take you from Detroit to Chicago on the same number of engine revolutions that the ordinary car of the same horsepower would require to travel from Detroit to South Bend.

It's doubtful that anyone actually stopped to figure out the difference in mileage between Chicago and South Bend, but the point was well taken; fewer revolutions per mile meant less wear on the engine and less fuel consumption.

Also noted on a rather extensive list of improvements for 1939 were two new safety features, push button door locks, which were conveniently installed at the corner of the garnish moldings on each door; and flush-mounted instruments and dashboard controls.

A new, larger V-type windshield—4 inches wider than in 1938—afforded drivers a clearer view of the road, while their comfort behind the wheel was assured by Chrysler's famous deep-cushioned "chair-high" seats, and an extra measure of legroom.

The most obvious new feature for 1939, however, was the conspicuous absence of the gearshift lever protruding through the floorboard. Chrysler's introduction of Steering Wheel Gearshift was a true benchmark in interior design. Highlighted in Chrysler sales literature, the column shift was acclaimed as the best single motor car improvement in recent years. Wrote Chrysler:

At last, the comfort of a third passenger in the front seat has been given respect and consideration. No longer need he straddle a wobbly gear shift lever—never again need he squeeze over against the right side passenger to give the driver elbow room for shifting.

The column-mounted shifter was standard equipment on Imperials and Custom Imperials, and available as an option throughout the entire 1939 model line.

Chrysler engineers were intent on finding new ways to simplify the driving experience, and in 1939 they added yet another new feature to the Imperial line, the "Fluid Drive" liquid clutch. It was basically a very simple design, consisting of a pair of turbine fans running against each other in an oil bath. Hooked between the flywheel and the standard clutch, it allowed the driver to leave the transmission in one gear and start and stop without having to depress the clutch. "Fluid Drive" was offered as an option on all eight-cylinder models and as standard equipment on the Custom Imperials.

Amid this seemingly endless array of new features being offered for 1939, Chrysler also managed to add a new series of cars, the New Yorker and Saratoga models, and a very limited production run of semicustom coupes built for Chrysler Corporation by the Hayes Coachbuilding Company of Grand Rapids, Michigan.

Cataloged as a Hayes Victoria Coupe, only 1,000 were built, with production of the semicustom bodies divided between the Chrysler, DeSoto, and Dodge Divisions. Within the Chrysler line, the share was split between the Royal and Royal Windsor, Imperial Eight, New Yorker and Saratoga series. Nineteen thirty-nine

was the only year Hayes produced the Victoria Coupes for Chrysler.

The body style was offered in the Gold Seal Six-Cylinder Chrysler Royal and Royal Windsor lines, priced at $970 and $1,035. A total of 255 of the 1,000 bodies were designated for this series, with 16 of that number built for export. Within the all-new 1939 Saratoga and New Yorker lines, only 99 New Yorker Victoria Coupes and 134 Saratogas were produced. At $1,395, the New Yorker was the most expensive version

Ralph Roberts had worked at LeBaron when Ray Dietrich conceived the idea of a dual-cowl phaeton in the late 1920s. The design stuck with him throughout his career, and the DCP was also a LeBaron favorite. When Roberts designed the 1940–1941 Newport for Chrysler, he took the dual-cowl phaeton to its final evolution by streamlining Dietrich's original concept.

The front end styling of the Newport was a streamlined version of the 1940 Chryslers, but tempered with a touch of Cord and the handsome redesign of the fabled Gordon Buehrig coffin nose by stylist John Tjaarda for the 1939 Hupmobile Skylark and 1940 Graham Hollywood.

The Newport's twin cockpits had fold-down windshields, just like the classic dual-cowl phaetons of the 1930s, and rearview mirrors for the rear occupants!

of the Victoria Coupe offered. Virtually a special order model, the Imperial Victoria Coupe was priced at $1,160, some $37 more than the standard Victoria.

Although the innovative shape of the Airflow had been too radical of a departure from contemporary styling trends, many of the breakthrough streamlining principles pioneered in 1934 influenced the design of Chrysler's 1939 models. As a result, the new cars had an unmistakably modern look about them—with contoured headlights built into the fenders, concealed luggage compartments (built-in trunks), narrower running boards, and a unique two-piece grille treatment that focused attention on the hoodline as never before. Perhaps in comparison to the Airflows the new body styles appeared somewhat subdued, but held up against competitive models for 1939, the new Chryslers were cutting edge designs, inside and out.

As in past years, the Imperial line was split into two series—the Imperial, Series C-23, and the Custom Imperial, Series C-24. For 1939, both models used the 323.5-cubic-inch straight eight, which was rated at 132 horsepower and 138 horsepower, respectively.

The restyled 1939 models gave way to all-new designs in 1940, the last that Walter P. Chrysler would live to see. On August 18, he died at his Long Island home after a long illness.

The 1940 Chrysler product lines were the most diversified yet, with cars, makes, and models to suit the smallest budget, or satisfy the most discerning of customers. Styling was generally similar among all four divisions, and every trace of the 1930's "classic" look had vanished. Wheelbases were longer, DeSotos more glamorous, Dodges sportier (later to become one of the all-time favorites of car collectors and hot rodders), and Plymouth still held on as one of America's all-time best sellers, delivering over 420,000 cars in 1940.

Chrysler Corporation ended the prewar era delivering 773,665 cars and trucks, with Plymouth 3rd in new car sales for the nation, Chrysler 9th, and DeSoto in 10th place.

KEEPING UP THE PACE

In 1941 Chrysler had the highest public visibility of any American automaker, being chosen for a third time to provide the Pace Car for the Indianapolis 500 Memorial Day classic. However, this time rather than selecting a production model, Chrysler chose one of its new "idea cars," a hand-built LeBaron dual cowl phaeton with

The Thunderbolt was designed as a sports car (albeit a large one) with seating for two and a retractable convertible hardtop.

streamlined coachwork. It was to become the first non-production Pace Car in history to lead the starting grid at Indianapolis. Known as the Chrysler Newport, the sporty twin cockpit phaeton was designed by Ralph Roberts and built by LeBaron. It was one of two stunning concept cars displayed by Chrysler Corporation in 1940.

The second car was the Thunderbolt, an aerodynamic, envelope-bodied two-seat hardtop convertible designed by former Cord stylist Alex Tremulis. One of the first designers to actually be called a futurist, Tremulis had joined Briggs (LeBaron's parent company) after the collapse of E. L. Cord's automotive empire in 1937. The Thunderbolt was the more advanced of the two 1940 concept cars, featuring a fully functional one-piece hardtop that retracted automatically into the trunk. (So if you think Ford had the idea first with the Skyliner, think again!)

Chrysler built six Newports and Thunderbolts in 1940–1941. Ironically, had they been produced in the 1930s, rather than in the 1940s, they would have been regarded as full customs, but by 1939 ordering a coachbuilt

The Thunderbolt had a very modern interior with leather upholstery and an aircraft-style instrument panel. Note the push-button radio, which is positioned sideways in the dash. This idea would appear again in 1963, on the Chevrolet Corvette!

car was a luxury few Americans could afford. The Newport and Thunderbolt were regarded instead as *concept cars* and were among the first to be shown by any American auto maker. (In 1938, Harley Earl designed a GM concept car known as the Buick Y Job. It toured the major American auto shows in 1938, and is the first known example of a concept car to be publicly displayed.)

The six Newport dual cowl phaetons featured streamlined aluminum bodies with aircraft-style cockpits front and rear, and dual folding windshields. Both the Newport and Thunderbolt utilized Gordon Buehrig's innovative hidden headlamp design, popularized on the Cord 810. The Newport's front end in particular had a great deal of similarity to both the Cord and John Tjaarda's redesign of the car, which was commissioned in 1938 by Hupmobile for its new Skylark models. The Hupps were face-lifted, rear-wheel-drive versions of the Cord 810 and 812, manufactured from the old tooling which had been purchased from the defunct Indiana automaker by Hupmobile for $45,000. (Graham also produced a similar version of the car in 1940 and 1941 known as the Hollywood.)

Of the two Chrysler show cars, the Thunderbolt was the real "concept" with an envelope body and fully integrated fenders, a design that was nearly a decade ahead of its time.

The Newport and Thunderbolt utilized conventional New Yorker running gear and the 128.5-inch-wheelbase C-26 chassis. Under the hood, however, Chrysler opted for the potent 143-horsepower, 323.5-cubic-inch straight eight used in the C-27 Crown Imperial. This was especially important for the Newport, which had to maintain a high rate of speed to set the pace lap at Indianapolis.

LeBaron Detroit built the Newport and Thunderbolt bodies and designed the richly appointed interiors. Overall, they were production quality automobiles and could very easily have been built in greater numbers. Chrysler sold all 12 cars in 1941. Today there is one example of each on display in the new Walter P. Chrysler Museum in Auburn Hills, Michigan.

The 1941 model year marked a turning point for Chrysler with the all-new Town & Country wagon, a styling innovation created by David A. Wallace, then president of the Chrysler Division. The wood-sided wagon would become a staple of the Chrysler product line throughout the 1940s, and in 1946, Town & Country styling would help launch Chrysler into the postwar era.

With Plymouth continuing to hold the number three position in the nation, selling 542,610 cars in 1941, Chrysler Corporation had a record-setting year. DeSoto delivered 97,497 cars; Dodge made 237,002

For 1942, Chrysler restyled the DeSoto line and equipped the new models with concealed headlights (compliments of the Newport and Thunderbolt concept cars), making DeSoto the first automaker to offer this feature since the 1937 Cord 812.

Chrysler scored another first in 1941 by providing the first nonproduction car to ever pace the Indianapolis 500. The 1941 Chrysler Newport was a streamlined version of the classic dual-cowl phaeton design. A total of six examples were built.

Americans new owners; and Chrysler turned over the keys to 161,703 automobiles. When the books were closed on the 1941 model year, Chrysler Corporation had sold over one million new cars!

For 1942 Chrysler restyled with sleeker, longer body lines, concealed headlights on DeSotos (compliments of the Newport and Thunderbolt concept cars), a sportier look for Plymouth, a fastback Town & Country wagon for Chrysler, and a new front end design for Dodge.

All four model lines were out of the chute with a bang for the 1942 model year and well on their way to setting new sales records when Japan staged a dawn raid on Pearl Harbor in December, plunging America into the throes of World War II.

In 1942 America turned its industrial might to the war raging in Europe and the Pacific, and automobile production came to a sudden and almost startling halt. The shortened 1942 model year, which ended in February, left Chrysler Corporation with total sales of 281,550 cars and trucks. Within months Chrysler had brought its full production strength to bear for the war effort, tooling up for the manufacturing of tanks, anti-aircraft guns, aero and marine engines, radar units, and the fuselages for B-29 Superfortress bombers.

Unlike Packard, Ford, and General Motors, all of whom had been involved in the arming of American forces during World War I, this was all new to the men and women of Chrysler. Their efforts were perhaps even greater felt because for the first time in the company's history, Ford, GM, Packard, and Chrysler were all on the same team, working together to build the arsenal of democracy.

Hollywood loved DeSoto. In the late 1930s, DeSotos were regarded as affordable yet attractive cars. Here legendary animator Walt Disney is seen with his brand new 1939 DeSoto sedan.

In what was one of the quickest construction projects in Detroit history, by the end of 1941 Chrysler had constructed the Detroit Tank Arsenal and was turning out five General Grant M3 tanks per shift.

Chrysler produced the M-4-A4, also known as the Sherman Tank.

CHRYSLER GOES TO WAR ON THE LAND, IN THE AIR, AND AT SEA

Whenever you hear someone say, "Boy, those big Chryslers from the 1970s were really tanks," remind them that during World War II Chrysler made tanks. Chrysler knows tanks, and a 1973 Imperial is no tank.

Tanks were Chrysler Corporation's number one wartime priority, and they rolled off the Detroit assembly lines with the consistency of Plymouth sedans—25,507 of them from 1941 to 1945. Chrysler production ranged from the General Grant M3 tank and the Sherman 32-ton tank, to the mighty 43-ton Pershing. By the end of 1941, each eight-hour shift at the Chrysler Detroit Tank Arsenal was completing five M3 tanks. But that wasn't all that came rolling out the doors of Chrysler Corporation assembly plants. At the same time, Chrysler was also producing marine engines (a total of 29,000); Navy personnel boats (built in conjunction with Gar Wood Boat Co. of

Marysville, Michigan); Sperry Gyro-Compasses, used to guide ships at sea; a variety of small harbor tugs, and the "Sea Mule," an almost indispensable tug that could do everything from pushing barges to transporting soldiers and gear.

Chrysler also built Bofors antiaircraft guns, which could be mounted on vehicles, on trailers towed behind Jeeps, and onboard ships, either individually or in pairs, in which case they were called pom-pom guns for their alternating firing pattern. During the war, Chrysler produced 30,095 Bofors and 14,445 pom-poms.

Chrysler was not only contributing to American military might on the land, and on the sea, but in the air as well. During the war, the Dodge Division turned out 18,413 Wright Cyclone nine-cylinder aircraft engines for use in the B-29 Superfortress bombers. Chrysler also produced the nose sections for the B-29, and components for the Curtiss Helldiver, the torpedo dive bombers made famous by Hollywood in World War II movies.

While civilian automobile production had been suspended after February 1942, Chrysler was still manufacturing motor vehicles for the military, and during the war delivered 438,000 Dodge, Plymouth, and DeSoto Army trucks of various sizes, ranging from 1/2-ton 4x2s and 4x4s to 1 1/2-ton 6x6s. In 1939 Chrysler had also completed a government contract for 25,000 Army trucks, so there were probably more Chrysler-built trucks in World War II than any other make, with the exception of Jeep, which Chrysler owns today. (Retroactively, Chrysler holds title to the most vehicles used in the war by U.S. armed forces.)

Another offshoot of Chrysler's war effort was the manufacture of munitions—3.25 billion rounds of small arms ammunition (.30 caliber carbine and .45 ACP), 328,000 explosive rockets, 101,000 incendiary bombs, and just under 2 million 20-millimeter shells. Overall, Chrysler Corporation's contribution to the war effort was one of the greatest of any American automaker.

When the war ended in August 1945, Chrysler was one of the first manufacturers to get automobiles back into production, and since Dodge, Plymouth, DeSoto, and Chrysler had redesigned their cars in 1942, a quick face-lift was all they would need for the 1946 model year. But Chrysler decided to do more than that. Much more.

Tanks for the memories. Chrysler workers pose for publicity photos at the Detroit Tank Arsenal. By 1945 Chrysler Corporation had produced over 25,000 tanks.

The Chrysler "Sea Mule" was one of the most versatile crafts in the Navy. It was manufactured in several configurations, the largest of which could be taken into open sea. The rugged little boats could perform a variety of tasks and were outfitted as tugs, used for ship-to-shore service; and another version known as a Harbor Utility Tug (HUT) was designed to be hoisted aboard larger ships to accompany the host vessel wherever it was sent.

CHAPTER 5

THE POSTWAR ERA BEGINS

Chrysler goes to town ... and country

There is nothing more exciting than a brand new car. And after World War II, Americans were frantic for new cars. Nothing had come off a Detroit assembly line in four years that didn't fly, float, ford rivers, or have artillery attached to it.

The trouble was, if you wanted a new car in 1946, you either had to know someone in the business or your name ended up at the bottom of a very, very long waiting list. There were no discounts, and there was no bargaining. The demand for new cars so far outstripped production that the best deal was just

The model pictured, owned by collector George Cummins, is an early 1947 Town & Country sedan. The early cars can be distinguished by the contoured all-chrome roof rack. Later models had a wood luggage rack with chrome corners. A total of 3,994 were built from 1946 to 1948, with prices ranging from $2,366 in 1946 to $2,880 by 1948. The sedans were built on the 121.5-inch-wheelbase C-38 chassis, and powered by Chrysler's 114-horsepower L-head six. Of the nearly 4,000 Town & Country sedans built between 1946 and 1948, today a mere 115 are known to exist.

Although GM is credited with building the first hardtop (a steel roof without a supporting "B" pillar), Chrysler actually predated the 1949 Buick Riviera by three years with the prototype Town & Country hardtop. Only seven were built. The cars were essentially convertibles with the roof section from a production coupe welded in place.

The interior of the 1947 Town & Country sedan was originally upholstered in Bedford cord, but owner George Cummins had his car restored with the optional Highlander plaid upholstery that was offered by Chrysler on the Windsor and New Yorker series.

to get a car, and dealers were charging a premium by loading new models with outlandish options.

In a way, this garnishment was to the dealer's advantage, and not just financially. Detroit had nothing to offer buyers that wasn't warmed over from 1942, so the add-ons made the cars seem somehow *newer* in the customer's eyes. This was car-starved America. After nearly five years without a new model in dealer showrooms, people were willing to accept just about anything. In Detroit, automakers were all faced with the same problem—how to produce new cars from prewar tooling. Chrysler had an idea. Back in the 1920s and 1930s, American white ash, imported Honduran mahogany, and other exotic woods were used extensively in the construction of coachbuilt cars, for the framework beneath the body, instrument panel fascias, door trim, and often the fine cabinetry and appointments that graced the rear compartments of town cars and limousines. In 1941 Chrysler had introduced a new model called the Town & Country station wagon, with a body partially built of ash and mahogany trim. Why not take the same approach with sedans and convertibles?

Both Ford and Chrysler hit on the same idea in 1945 and immediately began setting up for the 1946 model year. Although the Ford and Mercury Sportsman convertibles were successful, they paled in comparison to the popularity of Chrysler's Town & Country series, available in both sedan and convertible versions. The

Town & Country was perhaps the most noteworthy car of the immediate postwar era.

Chrysler had originally considered building an entire range of T&C models, including a two-door brougham, a roadster, a hardtop, and a convertible. Chrysler built seven prototype two-door hardtops (essentially a convertible fitted with a lengthened steel top from the standard Chrysler coupe) and one prototype Town & Country brougham. In the end, however, only the sedan and convertible made it into production. Even the venerable wood-sided station wagon introduced in 1941 was eliminated from the Town & Country line, and would not reappear until 1949. It seemed

to matter little, however, as buyers signed up to purchase the uniquely styled ash and mahogany-bodied convertibles and sedans almost as quickly as Chrysler could manufacture them.

The 1946 Town & Country convertible was built atop the C-39 series 127.5-inch-wheelbase chassis and powered by the 135-horsepower flat-head Spitfire Eight. The companion four-door sedan was mounted on the C-38 series 121.5-inch platform and equipped with the 114-horsepower L-head six. Chrysler also offered a one-year-only production run of 100 C-39 Spitfire Eight sedans in 1946, produced on the longer 127.5-inch chassis. With a base price of $2,718, it was some $350

A late-1949 model, owned by Robert Turnquist, does not have the mahogany decals. By now only the ash framework remained to distinguish Town & Country models.

more than the C-38 model, and just slightly less than the T&C convertible, which started at $2,743.

The cars were quite literally rolling furniture. Wood for the Town & Country bodies was hand-assembled in the traditional tongue-and-groove fashion used by furniture makers. Pekin Wood Products in Helena, Arkansas, a subsidiary of Chrysler Corporation, produced the white ash and mahogany body panels and framing, while Briggs body company assembled the steel body parts. All of the parts were then shipped to Chrysler's Jefferson Avenue plant in Detroit for final assembly.

The complicated and time-consuming manufacturing process had one major drawback: the Town & Country cost too much to make. The retail price was significantly higher than similar steel-bodied models, and they were vastly more expensive to repair, requiring both the skills of a body man and a woodworker.

The cost of the ash framework used on 1946 models, which extended from behind the cowl all the way to the rear bumpers, outlining the decklid and fenders, combined with the hand-applied mahogany veneer plywood covering the door panels and rear quarter panels was just too exorbitant, and late in 1947 Chrysler replaced the mahogany trim with simulated wood Di-Noc decals.

It took Chrysler Corporation until 1949 before a completely new line of automobiles was readied for introduction,

We've heard of cars with dual horns, but this is ridiculous! Actor Leo Carillo, best known as the Cisco Kid's sidekick, Pancho, had his 1947 Chrysler Town & Country slightly modified. The biggest problem Carillo had with the car was mooing violations.

In 1950 the convertible was gone, and a new Town & Country Newport hardtop model was introduced. Produced for only one year, a total of 698 were built. The Newport had an exclusive all-steel body with white ash framework. The side panels were painted body color, as they had been on late 1949 Town & Country models.

When Chrysler rolled into the 1950s, the power was on. In 1951 the New Yorker, equipped with the 180-horsepower Fire Power hemi, was one of the hottest cars on the road.

Chrysler's high-performance New Yorker convertible was chosen to pace the 1951 Indianapolis 500. Only 2,200 New Yorker convertibles were produced in 1951 and 1952. With the highest horsepower rating of any American production car, the New Yorker commanded a price of $3,941 in 1951 and $4,118 in 1952.

but during the period from 1946 to 1949, the Town & Country served Chrysler well as an image builder. The wood paneling gave Chrysler's first postwar models a significant advantage over other makes, and through 1948, Chrysler sold 8,368 Town & Country convertibles along with 4,049 six-cylinder sedans, and 100 eights.

As the new 1949 Chryslers began to arrive in dealer showrooms the demand for the Town & Country was beginning to ebb. By now, the word was out that however attractive they may have appeared, the wood-sided Chryslers required extensive care. Garaging a Town & Country in foul weather was almost as important as changing the oil and keeping the radiator filled. The notion of calling them land yachts was less a compliment and more a caveat about the fastidious attention these cars would require. It was recommended that the wood be treated the same as the planking of a yacht. It was to be given a fresh coat of varnish whenever it became dull or weathered, a long and tedious process which Chrysler recommended be done every six months to ensure a long lasting finish and protection from moisture. This has contributed to the Town & Country's staggering attrition rate over the past 50 years.

Exterior styling changes for 1949 were less than significant, compared to the renovations from Ford and General Motors, and Chrysler continued to offer the same engines it had introduced in 1942. The eight retained its rating of 135 horsepower, while the six was modestly increased to 116 horsepower. The Town & Country was still the most stylish model Chrysler had to offer, and perhaps the best looking car of the late 1940s.

Early 1949 models still had the Di-Noc decals, but Chrysler was soon turning out Town & Country convertibles with only the ash framework and painted body panels, a styling departure that would continue into 1950.

The 1949 models were changed substantially throughout the production run, and in fact, the earliest 1949s were actually 1948s. Explains collector Robert Turnquist, "Chrysler had a strike when the 1949 models were being built, so what they had left of the 1948s were listed as 'Series One' 1949. After the strike, the all-new 1949 cars were introduced." Turnquist's T&C was built toward the end of production, serial number 7410866. "The highest number listed is 7410995."

The 1949 Town & Country convertible was lavishly appointed throughout and with Chrysler's one-year-only grillework, a close runner-up to Cadillac when it came to front end dazzle. It was built on the C-46 chassis and considered part of the New Yorker series; only 993 were produced.

The 1949 model year would be the last for the convertible, and in 1950 the Town & Country would be offered as a Newport hardtop sedan, similar to the 1946 prototype, utilizing a steel top welded to a convertible body. Chrysler also had the contemporarily styled six-passenger Royal Town & Country station wagon. Only 698 Newports were sold in 1950, and when the 1951 models arrived in dealer showrooms, the Town & Country name only applied to the all-steel station wagon.

In the early postwar years, wood had given old models a fresh look and provided American automakers with the respite they needed to design and build completely new cars. With that accomplished, the time had come for the woodie to gracefully bow out of the picture. Another era had come to an end.

Even though all the hoopla in 1946 concerned the Chrysler Town & Country, DeSoto had a pretty impressive car of its own, the luxurious and large Custom Suburban.

By the time Virgil Exner had his hands on the styling controls, he was trying to figure out how to reverse the conservative trend that had given Chrysler's new 1953 models such a stodgy look. This top-of-the-line Custom Imperial was almost indistinguishable from the rest of the Chrysler line. Exner already had the fix with the Ghia Specials, but it would take several years before Chrysler styling could change direction.

CHAPTER 6

THE VIRGIL EXNER ERA

"They were just blown away by what they saw . . ."

Sometimes losing the war isn't all that bad. The United States has a long-standing tradition of helping its vanquished enemies rebuild their trampled landscapes and broken economies. It is part of being a responsible nation. In 1947, General George Marshall, who was appointed U.S. secretary of state, established the European Recovery Program, or as it is better known, the Marshall Plan. The following year, Congress allocated $17 billion to help rebuild war-torn industries throughout Europe. Tens of millions poured into Italy, which had perhaps been ravaged second only to Germany by virtue of being the ground upon which Allied and German forces chose to stage some of their most heated battles. Italy had been on the wrong side in the conflict, and geographically it was in the wrong place.

With one bold stroke, Virgil Exner changed the face of Chrysler and influenced a generation of Detroit automotive stylists. The 300C had a sporty profile with tapering, Flight-Sweep–inspired fins and scooped out wheel openings, thinner arch-shaped pillars combined with a large backlight, and a vast wraparound windshield. Still built on the New Yorker's 126-inch wheelbase, the 300C was only a half-inch longer than the original Chrysler 300. Its air duct brake-cooling system and new torsion-bar suspension were among the most important technical innovations in the industry for 1957.

Tan leather upholstery with vinyl front seat rear panels was standard on all 300C models. The leather had embossed pleats running side-to-side for cushion and back seat inserts. The 300C was offered with two transmission choices, the three-speed TorqueFlite automatic as standard equipment and a three-speed manual gearbox as part of the chassis-and-engine option package. The automatic had push-button controls on the left side of the dashboard.

Bombed by air, crushed by tanks, and trampled upon by millions of soldiers, it is remarkable that the Italian automotive industry was able to rebuild itself so quickly after the war. But Italy was always a country driven by its love of automobiles.

In the late 1940s, Chrysler Corporation was invited over to Italy by Fiat to assist in training its technicians in the latest American machining and assembly techniques. This process helped Alfa Romeo turn into a volume automaker in the early postwar years. In a very short time, Chrysler learned a great deal about the Italian auto making industry and the small but thriving *carrozziere*, which were among the last custom coachbuilding firms left in the world. A handful had also survived in England and France, but in America, custom coachbuilding was an art that had all but vanished.

Although Chrysler initially approached Ferrari coachbuilder Sergio Pinin Farina to build prototype bodies in 1950, by 1951 an agreement had been signed with Carrozzeria Ghia in Turin, which would build a series of cars based upon designs by Chrysler's chief stylist, Virgil Exner.

Exner was well seasoned, not only in design but in the politics of design, when he became Chrysler's chief of advanced styling in 1949. Previously, he had spent a decade working for Raymond Loewy, and was, in fact, one of the principal architects behind the Loewy

"image" as one of the world's great automotive designers. This ultimately led to a rift between the two legendary stylists. Loewy was loathe to give even the slightest bit of recognition to any of his collaborators—as far as he was concerned, the designs were by Loewy Studio, and that was that. This rankled Exner to no end.

At the time, legendary automotive stylist Gordon Buehrig was working with Exner on the Studebaker account at the Loewy Studios. Recalled Buehrig of Exner and Loewy's parting, "Exner was an excellent designer, and he was convinced that a job well done spoke for itself, on its own merits. Loewy, on the other hand, in addition to being a designer, was a promoter. He was good at selling his studio's products, and he was absolutely convinced that he could legitimately assume for himself the merits of anyone who worked for him." Exner finally grew weary of this practice, and in 1944 he quit and went to Studebaker with his designs. He virtually took the account away from Loewy and designed the South Bend, Indiana, automaker's landmark 1947 models.

These were the first postwar American cars to offer full-width envelope-type bodies and integrated fenders. For the era, they might as well have been props from a Buck Rogers serial. People were absolutely fascinated with the new Studebakers. In 1948 and 1949, Exner took their design a step further, after which he was personally recruited by Chrysler boss Kauffman Thuma "K. T." Keller to become head of the advanced styling studio.

Despite building a quality product, Chrysler had been burdened with a stodgy, old man's car image since the late 1930s. Keller (who had defected from General Motors back in 1926 to become Walter Chrysler's vice president of manufacturing) hoped Exner could change all that. A conceptualist who could develop character in a design, Exner was also shrewd enough to know he would need outside help to transform Chrysler. He turned to Carrozzeria Ghia to develop what he termed "idea cars," designs that Exner believed would take Chrysler a generation ahead of Ford and GM styling.

In many ways Virgil Exner was absolutely right. His Forward Look put Chrysler at the forefront of American automobile design in 1955, and it came about as a direct result of the Chrysler-Ghia relationship that began in 1951.

By taking advantage of the low cost of construction in postwar Italy, along with the atelier's fine craftsmanship, Exner and Ghia produced some of the most beautiful concept cars ever to flow from a designer's pen: the d'Elegance and Chrysler Specials, the DeSoto Adventurer II, Dodge Firearrow, and Chrysler Falcon, to name but a few.

The first Exner-Ghia designed Chrysler was built in 1951 on a 125 1/2-inch-wheelbase Saratoga chassis. The finished all-steel bodied car was shown to the Chrysler brass on November 2. It was named the K-310 (the "K" reputedly after K. T. Keller). This car was followed by the C-200 convertible, which was shown to the public on April 2, 1952, during the Parade of Stars Auto Show at the Waldorf-Astoria hotel in New York. The public response was exactly what Exner had hoped for, and a third series of cars was commissioned.

While the actual timeline is a bit sketchy, among the rarest models produced during the 15-year alliance forged between Chrysler and Ghia were the Exner-designed Ghia Specials manufactured from 1951 through 1954. The majority were built on the standard 125 1/2-inch-wheelbase chassis used on all Chrysler models except the Imperial in 1953. Powered by

Chrysler's 331-cubic-inch, 180-horsepower hemi V-8, Ghia models were equipped with either the new Power-Flite two-speed automatic, or the older Fluid Torque transmission, depending upon when they were built.

The maroon and white example shown, from the Houston, Texas, collection of Jerry J. Moore, was delivered in 1953. According to Chrysler archives, this is one of approximately six cars based on Exner's 1952 Chrysler Special and 1953 Thomas Special. The latter was commissioned by C. B. Thomas, then president of the export division of Chrysler Corporation. After building six cars for Chrysler, it is estimated that Ghia produced another dozen for itself.

The transatlantic relationship that formed between Chrysler and Ghia also brought forth a series of limited production models beginning in 1953 with the Chrysler Ghia GS-1 coupes, a series of 400 cars closely resembling Exner's 1952 Chrysler Special and sold exclusively in Europe by Societe France Motors. These were followed

Conceptualist, designer, and some say the savior of Chrysler in the early postwar era, Virgil Exner (pictured with the XNR Idea Car) joined Chrysler in 1949 as head of the advanced styling section. In 1953 K. T. Keller appointed him director of styling, and by 1957 Exner had taken Chrysler to the forefront of American automotive design.

The sports car–like styling of the Chrysler Ghias was a generation ahead of any American car in the early 1950s. Remember that the Chevrolet Corvette was only introduced in January 1953, and the first Chrysler Ghia had been shown a year before. Even by European standards, this 1953 Chrysler Ghia Special was as contemporary in appearance as a Ferrari 410 Super America.

by the limited production 1954 Dodge Firebomb cabriolet; the Chrysler-powered Dual Ghias, built from 1956 to 1958 by Dual Motors, Inc., a Detroit-based heavy truck manufacturer headed by wealthy enthusiast Gene Casaroll; and the imposing Chrysler Crown Imperial Ghia Limousines, manufactured from 1957 to 1965. Ghia would also build the bodies for Chrysler's experimental turbine cars in 1963.

GHIA'S STORIED PAST

Carrozzeria Ghia has had something of a roller coaster history, and a very colorful collection of owners who have paid the rent on the establishment's Turin design studio since the end of World War II.

In 1972, the Ford Motor Company became heir to the Ghia name and crest, which has since been splashed on everything from concept cars to the Ford Fiesta. Before that, the company was controlled by the stone-willed Alejandro de Tomaso of Mangusta and Pantera fame. But long before the lineage of owners took on international colors, everything from the body bucks and tooling, to the drafting tables and pencils, belonged to one man, Giacinto Ghia, and the cars he built in the *Turino atelier* were among the most exciting the world had ever known.

Founded in 1915 as Carrozzeria Ghia & Gariglio, the firm designed and built automobile bodies for many of Italy's most respected marques: Alfa Romeo, Lancia, Italia, and Fiat. The carrozzeria also gained a reputation in the 1920s and 1930s for building innovative, lightweight aluminum alloy sports car bodies. Ghia's design for the Alfa Romeo 6C 1500, in particular, received rave reviews from the European motoring press in 1927.

The design and construction of automobile bodies for both touring and competition had been Ghia's foundation for nearly a quarter of a century, when World War II brought an abrupt end to Italy's prosperous luxury car market and impassioned love of motorsports.

Although there were no automotive chassis on which to work, there was regular income for the Turin factory throughout the early years of the war, manufacturing carts for the Italian army and a line of very stylish bicycles. There seemed little for Giacinto Ghia to do but wait for the war to end. For Ghia, the end came late in 1943, when the entire factory was destroyed during an Allied bombing raid. The loss of his buildings and all of his tooling and designs was too much for Ghia to shoulder, and on February 21, 1944, he died of heart failure while supervising the reconstruction of the Turin factory.

Determined that the family name would continue, Santina Ghia offered what was left of her husband's company to two of his closest associates, Giorgio Alberti and Felice Mario Boano, a successor chosen by Giacinto before his death.

An accomplished coachbuilder in his own right, Boano had apprenticed at the Stabilimenti Farina and then with Pinin Farina before establishing his own *scoccheria*, an industrial carpenter's yard supplying coachbuilders, including Ghia, with the full-scale wooden bucks over which metal body panels are hand formed. It was in fact the very same business in which Giacinto Ghia had made his start. Whether it was their similar backgrounds or just that Ghia took an immediate liking to Boano, he had made it clear to all involved that he wanted Boano to head the carrozzeria when he retired.

Together, Boano and Alberti rebuilt the company from the ruins of the Turino workshops, and by the late 1940s had contracts for the design and manufacture of coachwork for Delahaye, Delage, and Talbot Lago, along with orders for traditional bodies from two of Ghia's oldest clients, Alfa Romeo and Lancia.

Although they were never unfriendly toward each other, Boano and Alberti did not get along, and often disagreed on how the company should be operated. The pragmatic Mario Boano brought an end to their disputes by

It was from Exner's styling influence that Ghia's best work evolved in the 1950s. One need only compare the 1953 Chrysler Ghia's stylish lines with the Alfa Romeo 1900 Ghia Coupe (pictured), which was shown at the 1953 Turin Auto Show. In the Alfa, Exner's influence is evident in the bold grille design flanked by large openings for the headlamps, an Exner technique that Mario Boano and his son Gian Paolo tastefully made their own.

The relationship that grew between Virgil Exner and Carrozzeria Ghia brought about some of the most dramatic design concepts of the early postwar era. The 1954 Dodge Firearrow (yellow car), 1955 Chrysler Ghia Falcon (silver car), and 1957 Chrysler Diablo all contributed to Dodge, Chrysler, Plymouth, and DeSoto's breakout styling in 1957. All cars from the Joe Bortz collection.

Even in 1954 Exner's use of tailfins to accentuate fenderlines was becoming evident. Each successive design would see higher fins and more dynamic fender treatments.

Dodge powered the Firearrow with a modified Red Ram V-8 developing 150 horsepower. The engine was coupled to a high-ratio torque converter with automatic transmission.

buying out Alberti in 1947, thus giving himself absolute control of the carrozzeria. Running the entire company was something of an eye-opener for Boano, who soon discovered that his place was in the design studio and not the front office. In 1948 he hired Luigi "Gigi" Segre, the former commercial director of SIATA (one of Italy's most respected tuners), to take over management of Ghia. Segre was one of those rare individuals endowed with both business acumen and a talent for design and engineering. He was both a blessing and a curse to Mario Boano, who sent Segre to America in 1949 to meet with Virgil Exner and Chrysler CEO K. T. Keller. The three quickly formed a friendship that would bond the American automaker and Carrozzeria Ghia S.p.A. together for more than a decade, but leave Boano almost an outsider.

In Virgil Exner, Segre had found a visionary with aspirations that could, and eventually would, make the alliance between the two companies one of the most significant of the postwar era, and help build Ghia's worldwide reputation. This had been one of the key issues Segre had argued about with Boano, who wanted Ghia to concentrate more on the Torinese automotive industry. Exner and his advanced styling group at Chrysler, which included Cliff Voss, Maury Baldwin, and consultant Paul Farago, who ran a specialty sports car shop on the outskirts of Detroit, were the guiding force behind the Chrysler Ghia designs. Farago, who was of Italian descent and spoke the language fluently, often acted as Exner's interpreter in meetings with the Ghia design staff.

Over the years Exner managed to keep himself on good terms with both Segre and Boano, despite their strong differences of opinion on the Chrysler-Ghia relationship. Late in 1953, the two men finally reached an impasse, and this time it was Boano who sold his holdings, giving Segre complete control of Ghia.

Ghia's association with Chrysler and Exner attracted many of the world's leading automakers to their Turino doorstep, and soon the carrozzeria was designing concept cars and producing coachbuilt bodies not only for Chrysler, but also for Ferrari, Jaguar, General Motors, and Ford.

It was from Exner's styling influence, however, that Ghia's best work evolved in the 1950s. One need only compare the 1953 Chrysler d' Elegance to Ghia's stylish Alfa Romeo 1900 Coupe, shown at the 1953

Described by Chrysler as a "competition-type sports roadster," a total of three Ghia Falcons were built in 1955, all on modified 105-inch-wheelbase production car chassis. Had Chrysler put the Falcon into limited production, it would have been a worthy competitor to the 1955 Corvette and Thunderbird.

Turin Auto Show, to find the unmistakable styling cues. In the Alfa, Exner's influence is evident in the bold grille design flanked by large openings for the headlamps, an Exner technique that Mario Boano and his son Gian Paolo tastefully made their own. Contours similar to the 1952 Chrysler Specials are also evident in the curve of the Alfa 1900's roofline and in the outline of the backlight.

The greatest spinoff ever of Exner's Chrysler Ghia designs (in truth, the outright thievery of the design by Ghia stylists) was the Volkswagen Karmann-Ghia, introduced in August 1955. The Karmann-Ghia was a scaled down version of the Chrysler d' Elegance combined with several early Ghia coupes that lent sports car style to one of the world's most trendy automobiles.

A TRANSATLANTIC RELATIONSHIP

The relationship that developed between Chrysler and Ghia in the 1950s contributed to the sharing of ideas and designs that traveled in both directions across the Atlantic, creating cars that were neither American nor Italian in design and execution, but something new

The Falcon's interior was production car quality, a simple but sports-minded design with a decidedly Italian influence.

Chrysler spent an estimated $250,000 to develop the Dart into a test lab on wheels, piling on more than 85,000 miles to evaluate aerodynamics and its effects on handling. After a trip back to Italy in 1957, the Dart returned stateside with its retractable roof removed, the fins trimmed down, and a new name, Diablo.

The most modern of all the Chrysler Ghias, the Diablo roadster featured a luxurious, high-tech interior with every accessory then imaginable, including air conditioning.

and wonderful. Something we might take for granted in today's era of international design, engineering and manufacturing, but in the 1950s, the Chrysler Ghias were unique in all the world.

The Ghias gave Exner the opportunity to create a new school of design in Detroit. In the postwar era, Chrysler was once again at the forefront of American automotive styling with the Chrysler-Ghia Idea Cars, the Forward Look, and trend-setting 1957 Chrysler 300C. Seemingly overnight, Chryslers had sprouted tailfins, bold grilles, and youthful, athletic lines that set them apart from anything being built in Detroit.

Virgil Exner had set the stage for Chrysler's styling renaissance back in 1949. "Our cars are not of the future," he said, "but new idea cars exploring excitingly new workable areas of styling and design." DaimlerChrysler Executive Vice President Tom Gale, the man most responsible for Chrysler's current streak of styling genius, says, "When I look back at the 1950s, I realize that there were some incredible breakthroughs. Virgil Exner's contributions to Chrysler during that era were very significant. I think if you go back and talk to guys like Chuck Jordan, who at the time was a young GM designer just starting out under Harley Earl and Bill Mitchell, they were dramatically affected by what Exner did. I remember Charlie telling me a story. It was late 1956 and the GM guys hadn't seen anything on the new Chryslers, so they went down to the Chrysler lot to look over the fence and see what was going on. They were just blown away by what they saw. It was a Chrysler 300C. From that moment on, Exner had a profound affect on everyone in Detroit."

Chuck Jordan, who retired in 1992 as vice president of design for General Motors, agrees. "In the 1950s, people were anxious, fascinated by what was going to happen in cars. After the war, we only had face-lifted models to fill the gap, and everybody was waiting for that new generation of cars to come along. However, that really didn't happen in the early 1950s, at least not as a great emotional statement, until the 1957 Chryslers came out." No one, however, summed up the influence of Exner's dynamic Chrysler styling better than General Motors Vice President and Pontiac Division General Manager Semon E. "Bunkie" Knudsen who said, "You can sell an old man a young man's car, but you can't sell a young man an old man's car." That had been Chrysler's problem, and Exner had fixed it. He lit a fire under Detroit and the best and flashiest cars of the era came on the heels of the 1957 Chryslers.

Chrysler waded into the 1950s with a wide variety of models, but perhaps the most famous was the 300 series. It was everything an automotive enthusiast could ask for in a family car. The original Chrysler 300, like this example owned by Otto Rosenbusch, was the first production model to deliver a wheel-spinning 300 horsepower, with a 331-cubic-inch hemi V-8 under the hood.

BY THE LETTER

Have you ever wondered how an automobile, a complex amalgam of steel, fabrics, rubber, and metal castings, can be elevated in prominence from a mere means of personal transportation to that of a cultural icon? To become that important, to become a benchmark in history, a car must have a unique aura, something that grabs your attention, stirs the imagination, keeps you awake at night, or perhaps causes your thoughts to stray during the day. It must sow the seeds of avarice that render artifacts irresistible and turn otherwise sensible people into enthusiasts. Virgil Exner no doubt had this in mind when he created the Chrysler 300. However, it's doubtful that he planned for its popularity to last into the next millennium; more likely, his goal was just to get through the model year.

The original Chrysler 300 of 1955 had been the first full-fledged production model to deliver a wheel-spinning 300 horsepower when you dropped the hammer. Powered by a 331-cubic-inch Chrysler hemi V-8,

Chrysler revamped its pedestrian image in 1955 with the all-new C300. The "Banker's Hot Rod" of the era, the stylish but not overstated C300 was powered by a 300-horsepower hemi V-8. In its first year, the C300 virtually dominated NASCAR racing, beginning a Letter Car legacy in American motorsports.

The Chrysler 300 lineage spans more than four decades, beginning with the first 300 model in 1955 (left) and progressing through the 1950s and 1960s with outstanding examples like the 1960 300F and 1961 300G. At far right is the latest letter car, the 2000 300M, heir to a proud tradition of high-performance Chryslers. *Cars courtesy of Otto Rosenbusch, Octie Ham, John McMullen. Location courtesy Meadow Brook Hall, Oakland University*

The 1960 Chrysler 300F convertible is ranked as the number one letter car. Equipped with the optional 413-cubic-inch V-8, the 300F delivered a whopping 400 horsepower. Only 248 were built for the year.

the 1955 models were flat out hell on wheels. The stock V-8s had been modified with the addition of two Carter four-barrel carburetors and a solid lifter high-duration camshaft of the same grind American sportsman Briggs Cunningham used in his 1954 Chrysler Le Mans engines. The added underhood gear boosted horsepower from the stock 250 to that magic 300 number.

Throughout the 1950s, Exner's influence on Chrysler styling was equal to that of Harley Earl's at General Motors. Like the GM Motorama cars, Exner's Idea Cars at Chrysler helped to set design standards automakers both here and abroad would follow for more than a decade. The 1957 Chrysler model line was very likely the zenith of that trend. They were introduced under the guise of being models originally planned for 1960. The wedge-shaped 1957 Chryslers caught GM,

Ford, and the rest of the automotive industry completely off guard, with styling a full generation beyond that of Chrysler's landmark 1955 Forward Look. Indeed, the 1957 Chryslers bore no resemblance to their predecessors, or for that matter, any other automobiles on the American road. The greatest benefactor of Exner's bold new styling was the Chrysler 300C.

The origins of the 300C clearly trace back to the Ghia designs. The Ghia Falcon and Chrysler "613" (300C prototype), both completed in 1955, gave rise to the final evolution of Exner's front end styling for 1957. The rakish bodylines and lofty tailfins were adapted from a pair of 1955 Idea Cars known as Fire-Sweep I and Fire-Sweep II, designed by Chrysler stylist Maury Baldwin. Combining Exner's "613" design, the Fire-Sweep concept cars shown at auto shows throughout

1955 and 1956 accurately forecasted the look of the all-new 1957 300C.

The "C" made its debut on December 8, 1956, at the New York Auto Show. From any angle, this was a car unlike any that had been offered by an American automaker. From the massive Ghia-inspired grille, consuming most of the front end—a basic theory of emotional relationship, i.e., the larger the grille the more powerful the car—to the dynamic tailfins, that for 1957 reached an unparalleled high, the 300C was more of a sensation than any competitive model offered by GM or Ford.

Behind the massive 300C grille, Chrysler's standard engine for 1957 was a 392-cubic-inch, 375-horsepower, Fire Power V-8 with special hardware, including mechanical tappets, stronger push rods, adjustable rocker arms, double valve springs, valve seat inserts, twin four-barrel intake manifold and carburetion, dual air cleaners, lighter-weight valves, hardened crankshaft, trimetal bearings, high-output camshaft, special piston rings, custom calibrated distributor, high-temperature spark plugs, and speed-limiting radiator fan.

For those desiring something more, an optional 390-horsepower engine-and-chassis package priced at $550 provided a more radical camshaft; 10.0:1 compression; limited-slip differential; 2.5-inch low back pressure exhaust system; heavy-duty clutch and drive shaft; a three-speed manual transmission; manual steering; and a choice of 13 different axle ratios that allowed performance to be tailored to any conditions of use. Although this package was primarily for professional racers, more than a few ended up on the street.

The 300C came with a three-speed TorqueFlite automatic as standard equipment. The automatic had push-button controls on the dashboard and the governor on the unit was recalibrated for the higher torque output of the 392 engine. On the 18 cars built with a stick-shift, a 1957 Windsor steering wheel was used, a cover was placed over the push-button control housing and the power steering, power brakes, and air conditioning features were deleted.

The all-new 300C had some big shoes to fill. In 1956 the 300B had become the champion of American stock car racing with 37 AAA and NASCAR titles, and an Unlimited Stock Class victory at Daytona.

Although factory-sponsored racing was on the decline by 1957, due to the competition ban instituted by the Automobile Manufacturers Association (AMA), driver Red Byron captured first place at the Daytona Safety and

The 300F had some rather interesting features, not the least of which were swiveling seats!

An optional V-8 displacing 413 cubic inches and equipped with a 30-inch Crossram induction manifold gave the 300F a full 400 horsepower and almost unchallenged possession of the American road. During the year, 300F models won the first six places in the flying mile runs at Daytona, with the winning car averaging better than 144 miles per hour.

Performance Trials with a new 300C, recording a top speed in the flying mile of 134.108 miles per hour.

Granted, the 300C wasn't quite as fast as the lighter, record-setting 300B driven the previous year by Tim Flock to a flying mile speed of 142.911 miles per hour and a two way "unofficial" stock car record of 139.9 miles per hour, but it was better looking by a wide margin and still the only full-size, six-passenger American car capable of cruising at 100 miles per hour.

Driving for Karl Kiekhaefer's Mercury Marine race team, Flock (who had a somewhat bizarre reputation, having on occasion carried along a chimpanzee as his co-driver) had established the world two-way average speed record at Daytona with the 300B in 1956, but since there was no actual class for this it was considered "unofficial." The bottom line was that no other stock sedan in the world, up to that time, had ever gone faster than the 300B. The 300C capitalized on that image, with dealers touting the new model as the fastest production car available in 1957.

Still built on the New Yorker's 126-inch wheelbase, the 300C was only one-half inch longer than the original Chrysler 300. Its air-duct brake-cooling system and new torsion-bar suspension were among the most important technical innovations in the industry for 1957. Torsionaire-Ride was hailed as a revolutionary system with torsion-bar front springs and ball-joint wheel suspension. Briggs Cunningham had used a similar setup on his 1953 Le Mans machinery and all Chryslers got it for 1957. The 300's system was special, with 40 percent stiffer bars to provide a race car type of ride. In combination with a revised front-end geometry and a low center of gravity, the 300C was the best-handling road car in America, not to mention the fastest. A total of 1,918 high-performance motoring enthusiasts were willing to step forward and plunk down $4,929 for a

Chrysler's 1961 model line brought tailfins to new heights, literally and figuratively. The 300G series continued the letter car's limited production status with 337 convertibles coming off the assembly line. This superbly restored example is from the John McMullen collection.

300C Coupe in 1957, and another 479 spent a whopping $5,359 to drive away in one of the limited production Chrysler 300C convertibles built that year.

For 1957 Chrysler offered five exterior finishes with a tan leather interior standard. A handful of cars were ordered with interior combinations not officially listed as options. These units received an "888" code designation which signified a nonstandard upholstery selection, rather than a specific color choice. Such cars are exceptional rarities today.

For 1958, the letter was "D" and production was down. The 300s were equipped this year with the 392-cubic-inch engine rated at 380 horsepower in standard trim, and 390 horsepower with an optional electronic fuel injection system produced by Bendix. The injected 390 was exclusive to the letter cars and only offered in 1958. It was a car clearly built for those whose sole desire was to humiliate Chevrolet fuelies at the local drag strip and turn the little girls' heads on cruise night.

For the year, Chrysler produced only 191 300D convertibles, and of those, only 35 were equipped with the 390. The coupes were almost as scarce a commodity, with orders for the 300D hardtops totaling only 618 cars.

Production was even more limited in 1959, making the Chrysler 300E one of the rarest of all letter cars. Only 140 convertibles and 550 hardtop coupes left the factory. This year the cars would be equipped with a new 413-cubic-inch V-8, developing 380 horsepower.

Beginning a new decade, the letter for 1960 was "F" and it stood for fantastic! An optional V-8, displacing 413 cubic inches and equipped with a 30-inch Crossram induction manifold, gave the letter cars a full 400 horsepower and almost unchallenged possession of the American road. During the year, 300F models won the first six places in the flying mile runs at Daytona, with the winning car averaging better than 144 miles per hour. At Bonneville, Andy Granatelli drove a supercharged version of the 300F to a two-way record with an average speed of 172.6 miles per hour, and his brother Joe set a record for the flying mile.

The "F" series convertible is ranked as the *number one* letter car, a beautiful piece of performance machinery priced at $5,766 in 1960. Sales for the year totaled 248, while the new hardtop coupes came close to the magic 1,000, ending the model year at 964 cars.

The 300F offered a list of options almost as long as the car itself (18.3 feet). Included were air conditioning, Electro Touch tuner or Music Master radio, power

antenna, remote side mirror, a Mirror-Matic inside rearview mirror which automatically adjusted at night for headlights, six-way power seats with dual swivel front buckets, tinted glass, limited-slip rear differential, the 400-horsepower V-8, and a manual four-speed synchromesh transmission. Adding a unique styling touch to the 300 series, the 1960 models also featured Chrysler's "Flight-Sweep" trunk lid, which sported a simulated spare wheel.

The standard engine for the 300F was a 90 degree V-8, utilizing a wedge-type combustion chamber, overhead inline valve design, high-output camshaft, and heavy-duty valves, springs, and dampeners. With a 10:1 compression ratio, the engine developed 375 horsepower. Equipped with a 3.31:1 rear axle, optional ratios from 2.93 to 3.73 were also available. Completing the car's designed-in performance was a special suspension with heavy-duty torsion bars, rear leaf springs, and

New canted headlights gave the 300G a striking appearance, with the fenderline tracing back from the headlamp housing to the tailfins.

shock absorbers. Add the 400 horsepower option, and by any standard of comparison, the cars were simply formidable, especially in a straight line. There was little else on the American road in 1960 that could hold its own against a Chrysler 300F.

Chrysler's 1961 model line brought tailfins to new heights, literally and figuratively. The 300G series continued the letter car's limited production status with 337 convertibles coming off the assembly line. Coupes, on the other hand, took an impressive jump in popularity, reaching 1,280 for the year. For their collectability, the "G" convertibles almost overlap the "F" series cars.

The early 1960s marked a turning point in Chrysler styling, with the design studio being handed over to former Ford stylist Elwood P. Engel. After a decade at Chrysler, Exner took his leave late in 1961, and opened his own independent design firm. His role at Chrysler had been one of the most important in the company's postwar history.

In a way, 1961 should have been the end of the letter car story. The following year, Chrysler shed the 300's exclusive image with the introduction of a new 300

Sport series. The *real* 300s were "H" models for 1962, but shared chassis and body styling with the new Sport series. Gone, too, were the fins and much of the unique character that had defined the 300 series. However, what it lacked in appearance, it made up for in sheer performance. The 300H came equipped with a 380-horsepower, 413-cubic-inch V-8, or an optional 426 that could be ordered in 373-, 385-, 413-, and 421-horsepower versions! There were probably more options for the 300H than there were customers in 1962. Only 123 convertibles and 435 coupes were built.

Chrysler rewrote the alphabet in 1963, skipping from H to J, and the convertible, which had become a little too "limited," was deleted from the model line. Less distinctive than ever, the 300J hardtop coupe only attracted 400 customers in 1963.

If the handwriting was on the wall, no one at Chrysler was letting on. In 1964 the 300K hit the ground with an optional 413 V-8, two four-barrel carburetors, a "Short Ram" manifold and 390 horsepower. Although output was the same as the previous year, this was now the most powerful engine available in any

The 300K hit an all-time high for letter car sales, with 3,022 hardtops, and after a one-year hiatus, 625 convertibles.

Chrysler model. The 300K hit an all-time high for letter car sales with 3,022 hardtops, and after a one-year hiatus, 625 convertibles.

For 1965 the letter was "L" and it stood for "last."

Chrysler completely redesigned its cars for 1965, spending more than $300 million on tooling. The new model line turned 1965 into a banner year for Chrysler, with production surpassing 200,000 cars. The new 300L hardtop coupes accounted for 2,405 sales and the 300L convertibles a total of 440.

In the end, the letter cars had become little more than badge engineered versions of the intermediate 300 series—the only 300s that would return in 1966. The breach in letter car production would span decades, until the introduction of the 300M in 1998, part of the company's return to the legendary Chrysler heritage.

The 300M, like its early predecessors, is a car dedicated to a single ideal: unique styling combined with exceptional performance. Even though there is only a six-cylinder engine under the hood (a hemi V-8 would be a wish beyond the dreams of avarice), it is one of the most powerful sixes on the American road: a 3.5-liter, all-aluminum, high-output, SOHC, 24-valve V-6 that delivers 253 horsepower at 6,400 rpm, and 255 lb/ft of torque at 3,950 rpm.

Driving the 300M, which walked away with the 1999 *Motor Trend* "Car of the Year" award, is an absolute treat. The beautifully appointed leather interior puts the driver in command of one of the best sports sedans to come from Detroit in years. The V-6 is coupled to Chrysler's AutoStick transaxle, which allows either automatic shifting or driver-selected manual shifts. The car's four-wheel independent suspension returns quick, agile steering response and provides virtually neutral handling characteristics. It is a car worthy of the letter "M". Magnificent.

The characteristic 300 grille has been somewhat subdued in the 300M. Ironically, the front of the more luxurious Chrysler LHS looks more like a contemporary 300.

CHAPTER 7

CHRYSLER MODELS FROM 1958 TO 1969

Big engines, cheap gas, and wild abandon

Chrysler and Virgil Exner had left everyone standing in the dust. At GM, Bill Mitchell and his staff were totally stunned by the high-finned 1957 Chrysler, Plymouth, and DeSoto models. Dave Holls and Chuck Jordan, then just young designers under Bill Mitchell and Harley Earl, couldn't believe what conservative Chrysler had done. In Dearborn, Lincoln Mercury chief designer Eugene Bordinat was less surprised, because Ford had already begun to design more daring cars, like the Continental Mk II and the Mercury Turnpike Cruiser. "We were pandering to the desires of the public," Bordinat said in a 1981 interview. "They wanted chrome and

The big fin look was used across the board at Chrysler, and even everyday family cars like this 1958 Belvedere looked sporty. This specific Belvedere was a dealer's display car that was never sold; it stayed on the showroom floor of Ray Rixman Plymouth in St. Louis until the 1959 models arrived. As implausible as it may sound, it was parked in a warehouse and forgotten about for the next 22 years! Now in a private collection, this is a totally original, unrestored car from 1958.

The Belvedere came equipped with the push-button Torque Flite three-speed automatic. The interior of this showroom display car was equipped with radio, and optional air conditioning.

fins and gadgets, and we slathered them with it, and the public thought it was great. From an aesthetic retrospect, it was tasteless, but I won't make any apologies for what we did back then. It was *in* for the day."

In 1957 the day belonged to Chrysler, and the momentum kept building throughout the remainder of the decade. The Imperial line was handily challenging the best Cadillac and Lincoln had to offer, and Exner and his personal staff, Cliff Voss and Bill Brownlie, had gone the crosstown rivals one better by designing the stunning Crown Imperial Limousine. Bodied in Italy by Ghia, the

cars were based on the new Imperial Southampton model but stretched to fit a longer 149.5-inch wheelbase.

Luxuriously appointed with interior styling, upholstery, and trim that had not been seen since the late 1930s, the 20-foot-long limousines commanded a staggering price of $12,000. At Cadillac, Mitchell had penned the Eldorado Brougham, which sent buyers reeling with a price of $13,074. The Cadillac and Chrysler made the Continental Mk II seem like a bargain at $10,000. None of them, though, had any great impact on the ledger sheet. Lincoln and Cadillac lost money on

The Chrysler-Ghia partnership reached its pinnacle with the 1957 through 1965 Crown Imperial Ghia limousines. The bodies were hand-built in Italy by stretching the Imperial Southampton to fit a 145.5-inch chassis. In 1957 only 36 examples were built. In 1958 the exclusive Ghia limousine was limited to 31, and in 1960, when the $16,500 model pictured was built, the number was a mere 16. In 1963 another 13 were built in the new body style on a stretched 149.5-inch wheelbase, 10 in 1964 and in 1965. The final 10 cars were built by Ghia in Spain for the 1966 model year, and that was the last of the Ghia Crown Imperial Limousines.

One of Plymouth's best-styled cars of 1957 was the Fury, which looked remarkably similar to the higher-priced DeSoto Adventurer. This was one of several contributing factors to DeSoto's landmark sales flop the following year. The Fury was priced at $2,925 while the Adventurer listed for $3,997. The Adventurer offered many more features, but the more affordable Fury dashed Adventurer sales. For 1957 DeSoto sold 1,950 Adventurers, while the Plymouth Fury finished the model year with sales of 7,438.

It was the best DeSoto of the postwar era at perhaps the worst time, at the start of the 1958 recession. The new Adventurer convertible was a striking counterpart to the Chrysler 300E and came equipped with DeSoto's new 361-cubic-inch, 345-horsepower Turboflash V-8. The car was also available with an optional fuel injection system, boosting output to 355 horsepower.

Listed as standard equipment for the 1958 DeSoto Adventurer were Torsion-Aire ride, Torque Flite push-button automatic transmission, power brakes, white sidewall tires, color sweep body treatment, instrument panel safety pad, steering wheel–mounted clock, and dual rear radio antennas.

every Mk II and Eldorado Brougham they sold, and Chrysler only delivered a handful of Ghia limousines in 1957 and 1958. Their real value was in image building, and for Chrysler in the late 1950s, *image* was everything.

In 1958 the American economy was struggling through the worst recession of the postwar era, and new car sales took a staggering plunge. Chrysler had its worst year since 1938, and division sales tumbled to a paltry 49,153 cars. Even with Plymouth, Dodge, and DeSoto factored in for the year, the numbers were not good. For the first time since the harrowing days of the Great Depression, the bottom line on the Chrysler Corporation's ledger book was written in red ink.

Chrysler styling continued to lead the industry in 1958 with Exner's big fins dominating the rear fenders of virtually every Chrysler Corporation model. In Detroit, it was as if a gauntlet had been thrown down, and Cadillac had picked it up. For the next two years, fins would rise until the GM luxury division built the towering 1959 models, which brought everyone back to their senses, and marked the beginning of the end for tailfins.

The last year of the 1950s marked another bold styling change at Chrysler. The high-finned Flight-Sweep look still made a Chrysler product identifiable from a block away, but grilles and rooflines were strikingly new, as were the engines under Chrysler hoods. For 1959 two new "wedge" engines were introduced to replace the long-lived hemis. Two versions were offered, a 383 V-8 delivering either 305 or 325 horsepower, depending upon options, and a hulking 413-cubic-inch V-8 pumping out 350 horsepower for the Imperial line, and a chest-swelling 380 horsepower in the new Chrysler 300E.

DeSoto offered what could only be called a counterpart to the Chrysler 300E, the sporty Adventurer model, which had been introduced in 1957 and modestly redesigned for 1958. An all-new convertible version made its first public appearance at the Chicago Auto Show on January 5. This was to be the most luxurious high-performance car in DeSoto's postwar history. It was also to be among the last. The division posted its worst sales year since the late 1930s, and when the belt had to tighten at Chrysler Corporation, DeSoto was destined to follow Packard, Hudson, and the Henry J down that long, lonely road from which there is no return. In 1960 DeSoto sales were a dismal 26,081 compared to Dodge's impressive 367,804, and by the end of 1961, the DeSoto signs were down at dealerships.

Chrysler was once again honored with the pace car duties for the Indianapolis 500. The car selected for 1963 was a new Chrysler 300 Sport series convertible. At the wheel is Indy Chief Steward Harlan Fengler.

Chrysler steamrolled into the 1960s with the most dramatic styling of any American automaker. The 1963 Imperial Crown Southampton was a striking exercise in unique design approaches. The prominent free-standing headlights were a page taken from the past and beautifully adapted to the present.

The last of the letter cars was the Chrysler 300L, which was barely distinguishable from the standard Chrysler 300 series. The 1965 models had all-new body styling and contributed to Chrysler's best year ever.

Chrysler had another record-breaking year in 1968. The new Chrysler 300 offered disappearing headlights built into the grille. The sporty convertible model was fashionable and fast, with a convertible top and a big 440-cubic-inch V-8 under the hood. It was priced at $4,337; Chrysler built only 2,161. The hardtop version was a best-seller, with 32,460 being sold for the model year.

INTO THE DECADE OF PEACE AND LOVE

Chrysler kicked off the 1960s with completely new cars, the first to feature unibody construction, even-bolder grilles, and the final evolution of the Exner tailfin, now strikingly canted away from the body with its leading edge extending all the way forward to the driver's door. It was an impressive design that once again set Chrysler styling well apart from Ford and GM.

While one could argue that Chrysler was marching to the beat of its own drummer, Virgil Exner, his days at the styling helm were numbered. The feeling was that Ex had done all he could, the 1960 models were a triumph, but the future belonged to a new generation. The Exner-Ghia relationship that had existed since the 1950s would come to an end in 1966, following production of the last Crown Imperial limousines.

After Exner's departure in 1961, the Chrysler styling department, now headed by Elwood Engel, made a complete change of direction and the cars began to take on a new, heavier look. Fins were gone in 1962 (except for the Imperial), and every trace of the Exner influence had evaporated by 1963. Exner did not take it well. He candidly referred to Engel's designs as looking like "plucked chickens."

For Chrysler, 1963 was a pivotal year. The completely redesigned models netted $161.6 million in earnings on more than $1 billion in sales. Much of this was due to Plymouth and Dodge each delivering nearly half a million new cars.

Powering Plymouth's near record sales was the compact Valiant line, which accounted for more than a quarter-million deliveries. Chrysler Division production reached 128,997 in 1963, a healthy indicator that the new body styling was on track.

At Indianapolis, a new Chrysler 300 Sport series convertible was chosen as the pace car for the 47th annual 500-Mile Memorial Day race, and Chrysler stunned the competition this year by announcing an unprecedented five-year/50,000 mile powertrain warranty on all Chrysler cars.

To cap off a remarkable model year, Chrysler debuted the Turbine, a futuristic sport coupe designed by Engel, built by Ghia, and powered by a 130-horsepower turbine engine. More than another concept car, the Turbine was put into limited production with a total of 50 examples built between October 1963 and October 1964.

The Chrysler Turbines were less radically styled than one might imagine and from the front looked very contemporary, almost like a Ford Thunderbird. From the rear, though, there was no mistaking the Turbine as something altogether different from any car on the road. It looked like a jet plane with taillights!

Over at Plymouth, performance is number one, and even the full-size cars have a robust look. The most popular was the Sport Fury "Fast Top." For 1968, 26,204 customers stepped up for the big Plymouth.

Dodge had a Rebellion going on in 1968, but Plymouth was just rebellious, building high-performance street cars like the GTX. Offered in coupe and convertible, the base engine was a 375-horsepower 440.

Although Engel's styling and Ghia's interpretation was anything but over-the-top, the turbine theme subtly worked its way throughout the car's entire design, from the round turbine bezels surrounding the headlights, to the turbine blade wheel covers and turbine-style shaft dividing the interior of the car.

The gear selector—low, drive, idle, and reverse—was mounted in the center console and designed like an aircraft throttle lever. It was surrounded by controls for the lights, windows, and accessories. The feeling in the cockpit was intended to be like that of an aircraft, and when the engine ignited, that is exactly what it felt and sounded like.

The whine of the turbine spooling up could turn heads for 100 feet in every direction, and on the road

there was the distinct trill of air rushing from beneath the car. While it was never so hot that blacktop melted from the exhaust heat (as so many urban myths about the car have proclaimed), the engine did run at 1,250 to 2,000 degrees Fahrenheit, and standing in the turbine's wake at idle was tantamount to that of a good sized leaf blower on a hot summer day. The engine idled at 22,000 rpm and redlined at a maximum 44,000 rpm. Driving the turbine was definitely an experience.

Although the Turbine's rated output was only 130 horsepower, that did not necessarily translate the same as it would from an internal combustion engine. The Turbine could go from 0 to 60 in under 10 seconds, and could have done it quicker if not for a classic case of

turbo lag, while the jet engine spooled up from idle. Theoretically, the car had no limit to its acceleration, other than the sheer physics of the body design which kept it down in the neighborhood of 120 miles per hour. That was a neighborhood few people were willing to visit in the hand-built prototypes.

Their purpose was to field test the feasibility of using turbines as an alternative to internal combustion engines. The turbines could run on anything from kerosene or jet fuel to 100-proof vodka. The only prob-lem was fuel economy. At best the cars averaged 11.5 miles per gallon, about the same as the author's 1999 Dodge Durango, and that was a key factor in keeping the Turbine from production. The 50 examples pro-duced were tested by 200 selected customers, who were given use of the cars for evaluation. The tests ran from 1963 to 1966, at which time they were returned to Chrysler. Most of them were dismantled, and a few, such as an example owned today by Frank Kleptz, were sold to private individuals or placed in museums.

The handcrafted Chrysler Turbine bodies were built in Italy, shipped to Detroit, and assembled on the Turbine chassis in a special Chrysler workshop. A total of 50 cars were built from October 1963 to October 1964.

Chrysler chief stylist Elwood Engel designed the body for the experimental 1963 Chrysler Turbine, and the designers at Carrozzeria Ghia, in Turin, Italy, gave it the finishing touches. Ghia produced 50 Turbine bodies. Today, only a handful survive and even fewer are running. This beautifully restored example owned by Frank Kleptz is driven almost every month and runs as well as it did in 1963, or better.

Take a close look at the instruments. The temperature gauge reads to 2,000 degrees Fahrenheit. As for the tachometer (far right), well, those numbers are not multiplied by 100—the x factor is 1,000! The redline is at 44,000 rpm.

Kleptz, who drives his Turbine regularly, still gets a kick out of the sound and the reactions of other motorists.

"It was a practical idea in many respects," notes Kleptz. "It drives very easily, and since the turbine is simply pushing air, the engine is almost vibration free. If not for the jet-like exhaust, it would almost be silent."

The majority of drivers who tested the Turbines registered the same complaints: poor fuel economy and lagging acceleration. Says Kleptz, "I really think that it might have been too odd back then for most people to get comfortable with."

The year 1963 was marked by changes, some great, some tragic, and a few that were unprecedented. Sidney Poitier became the first black actor to win an Oscar, the

film version of Henry Fielding's bawdy eighteenth century epic, *Tom Jones*, won for best picture—a hint, perhaps, that our conservative tastes were beginning to change. A new musical group from England with the rather unlikely name, the Beatles, started a meteoric climb up the charts that would change the very course of music in the mid–twentieth century. It was also one of the darkest years in our nation's history as we watched, in shock and disbelief, the assassination of President John F. Kennedy. For the first time since the advent of television, Americans were exposed to the full impact of the media—the awesome power to allow each of us to "be there." A grieving nation watched JFK's funeral, and the murder of accused assassin Lee

Not much to look at. The Chrysler turbine engine was nestled under the hood on a subframe. Mechanically, there was much less to it than a conventional internal combustion engine.

The Chrysler Turbine exhaled from underneath the rear of the car, out of sight and safe from an unsuspecting touch. With a running temperature of 2,000 degrees Fahrenheit, the Turbine's exhaust made 427 Cobra side pipes seem tame.

Harvey Oswald live on TV, and then again, and again, and yet again. It was a bitter taste of things to come.

By the mid-1960s, Chrysler was doing better than it had at any time in its history. In 1965 all-new body styling catapulted Chrysler past Cadillac for the first time in the postwar era, and the division broke an all-time record, delivering 224,598 new cars. Chrysler sales had never before surpassed 200,000 in a single calendar year. At the corporate level, Dodge sold 489,000 cars, and Plymouth delivered an unrivaled 726,234 cars.

Throughout the 1960s, Chrysler continued to expand its market share and introduce new and exciting cars with distinctive Chrysler styling cues and high-performance engines. By the end of the decade, Chrysler Corporation had virtually reinvented itself with new models, like the Dodge Charger, Plymouth Barracuda and Road Runner, sporty Chrysler coupes and sedans like the Newport, and posh Imperial Crown hardtop. By the end of the decade, the company had finally established itself as a true competitor to Ford and General Motors in every category and in every price class.

Walter Chrysler would have been proud.

CHAPTER 8

CHRYSLER CORPORATION FLEXES ITS MUSCLE

Meanwhile over at Plymouth and Dodge . . .

Back in the early 1960s, Bud Faubel enjoyed a reputation for consistently running some of the fastest Super/Stock cars in the nation. Bud's performance record dates back to his participation in the Daytona Speed Week Trials, where he established a record for NASCAR Class 6 automobiles with his 1961 Dodge wedge-head car, posting a speed of 144.17 miles per hour. He also competed in Class 7 with a Chrysler 300, establishing a new mark of 156.66 miles per hour, still one of the fastest times ever recorded by a stock car on the beach. A mild-mannered racer, Faubel was

Back in Virgil Exner's day, Chrysler's advanced styling was, well, advanced. Out of Ex's department came bold new concepts like the Chrysler Ghia Idea Cars, forecasting features that would evolve into production models like the 1957 Chrysler 300 and the Forward Look. That had pretty much changed by the flower-powered and politically turbulent 1960s, by which time concept cars were closer to Barris customs—in fact, some were actually built by George Barris—than to cars intended to give the public a glimpse into the future. Back in 1967, that glimpse was a Dodge show car called *Daroo II*.

The Chrysler-Dodge stylists had wanted a true roadster, so *Daroo II* had no top, no door glass, and no backlight. It seemed that practicality had gone out the window, or it would have if there had been any windows. A car that could have made the Duke Boys' *General Lee* blow a gasket, *Daroo II* was only 42 inches high with a chopped, frameless windshield, and featured a 15-inch-wide air foil–molded roll bar that connected via lengthy pillars to the rear deck lid spoiler. To accentuate the flat, trunkless rear deck, a raised panel with twin competition-style fuel fillers on either side ran the length of the car from the rear window opening back.

known as "Mr. Nice-Guy." The general manager of Shively Motors in Chambersburg, Pennsylvania, and one of several factory sponsored drivers for Dodge, he is best remembered today as the man who put the push-button transmission on the map in NHRA competition.

"I had about a dozen factory cars in the early 1960s," recalls Faubel. "Starting in 1960 I began racing wedge-head cars for Dodge and in 1964 I was the record holder in S/SA competition." Bud had set a time of 11.53-123.79 at Cecil County, Maryland, with his stage-three Wedge about the time Dodge engineer Tom Hoover came to him with a new idea, a hemi-powered drag car equipped with a push-button automatic transmission. "Hoover was head engineer for the Ramchargers, along with Jim Thornton, Dan Mancini, Mike Bucknel, and a brilliant young engineer by the name of Dale Reeker. It was about the middle of the 1964 season when they delivered the white Dodge 330 to our dealership. As I recall, it was one of the initial hemi drag cars and I believe the first one to be equipped with the automatic."

Faubel says that he initially tested hemis with both sticks and push-buttons and his 1964 wedge car was equipped with a push-button automatic. "The

Ramchargers had done a good bit of testing before putting the automatic in the hemi and their quarter-mile times had been consistently better with the push-button shifter than the stock three-speed. I think on the average you get better and worse with a stick," contends Faubel, recalling years of experience, "but the automatic was just plain better time after time, so I decided to give it a try in the hemi. It was something I'd never had before."

For competition, Faubel had the Dodge push-button changed to a manual shift. "We modified the valve body to make it work in a selective mode, but it still ran through a torque converter. You watched the tach, and when it got up in the high point of the horsepower curve, you'd hit the next button for the up-shift." Bud shifted at 6,500 rpm in each gear and got out of the quarter at about 6,700. "We left the gearing in the three-speed alone and changed the final drive and tires to match varying track conditions. On most quarter-mile tracks we were using a 4.56 ring and pinion or final drive. If the track was fast we'd use a 4.3. On a slow track we'd use a 4.89. That was a real screamer. It would get you going a lot quicker as far as ETs were concerned. It hurt a little bit on miles per hour, but you got there faster." As for rubber, most of the time Faubel stuck with M&H Super/Stock 7-inch tires on the rear and 5.60x15 Continentals up front, although on occasion he swapped the rears for 10-inch slicks.

The Dodge 330 Hemi Honker sedan got its distinctive nickname from Faubel's 1962 wedge car. Originally, a couple of Faubel's friends christened the 1962 Dodge during the Daytona Beach Speed Trials. "Marvin Panch, who'd won Daytona a couple of times, and Gale Porter, whom I worked with at Dodge in the early 1960s, were looking over my wedge car one afternoon and Gale wrote on the side of it with his hands in the dirt the word 'Honker.' It was an expression they all used for fast cars back then—'That car's really honkin!' they'd say. As for the goose, we added that to the 1964 hemi because it just sort of tied into the name as a symbol." After that all of the cars Faubel raced from 1962 through 1970 were called Honkers.

The hemi was pretty much stock says Faubel, "stock chassis and wheelbase, stock induction system, which was dual Holley four-barrel carburetors and a transistorized ignition."

The Dodge was handed over to Faubel and his own team of mechanics and the 426 hemi was prepared and blueprinted for Shively Motors by Jenkins Competition in Berwyn, Pennsylvania. "You were allowed to go .060 over," says Faubel, "so we bored the hemi out to around 430 cubic inches and that gave us roughly 600 horsepower with a 13.5:1 compression ratio. It was really a high compression car and you could tell it when you touched the accelerator, it spooled up instantly. In 1964 we were running it on Sunoco 104 octane fuel. We tried aviation gas a couple of times, but it really ran better on the Sunoco stuff and that was pretty much our fuel throughout the season."

The Honker took Faubel to the S/SA record for Super Stock Automatic class in 1964. "We were turning some pretty fast times," he recalls. The November 1964 issue of *Super Stock Magazine* listed the Hemi Honker's

record runs in 1964, including an 11.27-125.50 on 7-inch Super/Stock tires and an 11.09-125.52 cranked off on 10-inch slicks. Faubel and the Honker were undefeated throughout 1964. In fact, the NHRA record holder's only notable loss was at the NHRA Nationals at Indy, when Dodge engineer and racer Jim Thornton aced out the Honker with the Ramcharger's own hemi car.

The white Dodge 330 was a stripper with all of the windows, except the windshield, replaced with thin plexiglass. To reduce body weight, the front fenders, doors, door hinges, hood, front bumper, and bumper brackets were all aluminum, as were the seat channels for the twin buckets.

Faubel was a stickler for detail, and the Honker was about as stylish as a Super/Stock could get. Even when

It was about the middle of the 1964 season when race driver Bud Faubel took delivery of this white Dodge 330. It was one of the initial hemi drag cars and the first one to be equipped with the push-button automatic.

Behind the wheel of the Hemi Honker Faubel took the S/SA record for Super Stock Automatic class in 1964.

the rear seat was removed, the interior was meticulously reupholstered. "That's the way I wanted it," he says. "We always kept it nice looking."

In 1965 the Honker became Faubel's backup car, and in 1966 he sold it to a race driver in Altoona, Pennsylvania. "It ran a lot of local events for a couple of years and then was sold again. As with most race cars, it traveled down the road from one owner to the next until it finally disappeared. I don't think the car ever really got beat up much over the years. It pretty much had a charmed life," says Faubel.

He didn't see the Hemi Honker again until 1992, when it was shown in Carlisle, Pennsylvania, at the annual Chrysler meet. Owner Patrick McGroder had restored the car exactly as it was when Faubel raced it in the 1960s. McGroder's head restorer, Steve Banker, says that the car was located in 1984 through a broker in Colorado. It had been in a private collection in Colorado Springs for years. As Faubel had said, the Hemi Honker had a charmed life for a Super/Stock car. "It still had the original paint when we took delivery," says Banker, "and everything was there except the front bumper."

It took Banker about six months to complete a body-off restoration. "The car had never been wrecked and the only damage other than aging was the floorboard, which had been bent up a little when someone tossed the drive shaft." McGroder found a parts car and Banker simply drilled all the spot welds out from the metal floor section and replaced it. "It was really a nice car to restore because there weren't any alterations made to it from the time it was new."

As the centerpiece of McGroder's Factory Muscle Collection in Phoenix, Arizona, the Hemi Honker's 100 point restoration guarantees that it will likely never see the rubber patched tarmac of a drag strip again, other than for a photo session. Yet, sitting there in front of the Christmas tree it looks like a car that's still "honkin."

CUDA BEEN A CONTENDER . . .

Back in 1968, Chrysler engineers Tom Hoover and Dick Maxwell pulled a Barracuda test car from the Research & Development motor pool and proceeded to do something that hadn't yet been tried: they stuffed a

426-cubic-inch hemi engine under the hood. The result was a car that would launch Plymouth headlong into the muscle car era of the late 1960s and early 1970s.

The project actually had its beginnings in the winter of 1967, when Hoover, whose hand had been in every high-performance Plymouth project since the "Hyper Pak" slant six in 1961, got together with Dick Maxwell, the man whose responsibility it was to coordinate performance engineering efforts with the rules and regulations of the various racing associations, assuring Plymouth Super Stock cars were just that—*stock*. The project this time was to see whether a 426 hemi could be adapted to the new Barracuda, and if so, how long it would take to develop a Hemi Barracuda to run in NHRA's new SS/B class. As Hoover recalled in a 1968 issue of *MOPAR,* "Project Super/Stock not only went smoothly, but netted the corporation ownership of NHRA's SS/B class."

In 1968, Hoover wrote about the guideline that had been set down for the Barracuda project. "When we set out early last winter to build the drag car everyone was asking for, we had several general guidelines in mind. First, of course, were NHRA rules. Once past

them, they could, with minor modifications, compete almost anywhere. That was 1967.

"Second was cost. We wanted to build a car with a price that made sense. For instance, we could have put aluminum heads on the hemi to cut weight if we weren't thinking of economics, but it would have cost about $20 a pound for the weight we saved. We found cheaper ways to reduce the weight, and the car still fits in the 'B' class.

"Third, we had to make sure the car could be shipped conveniently, so we had to forego installing a racing cam and high-capacity oil pan because of driving and ground clearance problems that could develop at the factory."

As it turned out, the handful of production 1968 Hemi 'Cudas (around 55 cars) came with a "some assembly required" instruction manual. For one thing, the cars were painted only in primer, to allow individual customizing. Hoover and Maxwell had chosen orange and yellow for the Woodward Garage prototype, but when owners took delivery of their cars they were only "semifinished." Actually, less needed to be done to the 'Cudas than any other factory-built drag cars to come from a Detroit automaker, said Hoover. "To make it race ready, it needed only slicks, racing cam and valve gear, bigger oil pan and colors." Of course, that was after months of developmental work by Hoover and Maxwell on the hemi prototype, and some serious testing at

Interior was red vinyl and that was what Faubel wanted—a stock looking car on the inside. To the left of the dash were the buttons that did the trick. The special Hemi-Dodge transmission had a wider band on the kick-down gear to prolong life. Faubel modified the valve body so that each up-shift had to be made manually. Bud shifted at 6,500 rpm in each gear and got out of the quarter at about 6,700.

The Honker was powered by a "stock" 426 hemi bored 0.060 over to about 430 cubic inches, giving roughly 600 horsepower with a 13.5:1 compression ratio. Sunoco 104 octane fuel was mixed through dual Holley four-barrel carburetors.

The first hemi-powered Barracuda was built at the Woodward Garage by Tom Hoover, whose hand had been in every high-performance Plymouth project since the "Hyper Pak" slant six in 1961. The car was a stock Barracuda with a hemi engine stuffed under the custom-made hood.

Southern California's Irwindale Raceway in February 1968, where the Hemi Barracuda ran in the mid 11s.

On February 20, 1968, a memo was sent to all Plymouth dealers from R. D. McLaughlin, national sales manager, regarding the 1968 Hemi Barracuda Super/Stock:

"The Chrysler-Plymouth Division offers for 1968 a 426 Hemi-Powered Barracuda Fastback for use in supervised acceleration trials. Hemi-Powered Barracudas will be available through production in limited quantities in March. To order this vehicle use the Barracuda order form and specify Body Code B-029 and Transmission Code 393 for four-speed or Code 395 for automatic. No other specifications are necessary.

"Please note that the following items are deleted on this model: Heater, Body Sealer and Sound Deadeners, Silencing Pads, Outside Mirrors, Right Side Seat belt and Body Color paint. NO OPTIONAL EQUIPMENT OF ANY KIND CAN BE ORDERED.

"These vehicles will be sold without warranty and will display special stickers, which will read as follows: This vehicle was not manufactured for use on public streets, roads or highways and does not conform to Motor Vehicle Safety Standards. All customer orders must be accompanied by a signed disclaimer indicating

that the purchaser understands the above." The cost of a Hemi Barracuda was $5,495.

Less than a month before the memo was sent, Maxwell and Hoover had completed testing at Irwindale. The finished Hemi Barracuda had been pared down to a weight of just over 3,000 pounds with an engine rated at 500 horsepower, qualifying for the NHRA's new 6.00–6.99 pounds per horsepower SS/B and SS/BA categories.

To cut weight to a minimum, the hood and fenders were made of fiberglass, the front bumper was formed of steel that was only half the gauge used on the regular Barracuda, and the doors were acid dipped, to again reduce weight. Windows were made of Chemcor glass, which was only 0.080-inches thick but reputed to be as strong as thicker, heavier conventional glass.

Many of the performance parts used in the prototype and production Hemi Super/Stock Barracudas were carryovers from the extremely successful 1964–1965 hemi series, but shoehorning the hemi that had fit under the hood of a Dodge 330 sedan into the engine compartment of a Barracuda was more than a mere swap. The "K"-member had to be notched for pan clearance, then the whole engine had to be moved an inch-and-a-quarter to the right, giving breathing room all around. Fitting the engine became a game of dominos. The master brake cylinder had to be shifted forward and to the left, then the right front shock tower relocated, and the battery moved to the trunk. What remained was a car full of engine.

Carburetion for the 426 was by two four-barrel Holleys with 1.69-inch barrels all the way through on a dual cross-ram intake manifold. The setup was virtually the same as the one introduced by Plymouth on its 1965 Belvedere Super Stock. In contrast, the street hemi had two four-barrel Carters, with 1.44-inch primaries and 1.69-inch secondaries, on a conventional inline manifold. Compression was bumped to 12.5:1, a sizable jump from the street hemi's 10.25 ratio. The exhaust system was "simulated" with Hooker headers, pipes, and mufflers. Handling the heavy lubrication demands was a high capacity oil pump, and to keep engine temperatures below meltdown, a heavy-duty radiator and aluminum seven-blade fan with viscous drive were added.

Most of the characteristics of the 426 were familiar to enthusiasts who recalled special Plymouth drag products built in the early 1960s. In fact, there were no revolutionary innovations in the Hemi Barracuda to speak of, only time-tested features put together in one of the strongest packages to come out of Detroit for production drag racing.

Equipped with a four-speed manual gearbox, the prototype hemi carried a 10 1/2-inch-diameter hemi race clutch with a 0.300-inch steel housing, eliminating the need for a flywheel shield. The rear axle ratio was a heavy-duty 9 3/4-inch Dana 60, with a 4.89:1 ratio. On production cars equipped with the only available option, a manual shift TorqueFlite automatic, a high-stall-speed B&M torque converter was also added. Rear axle on the automatic was the 8 3/4-inch Belvedere version with a 4.86:1 ratio. As with the manual gears, the TorqueFlite was assisted by a Sure-Grip limited-slip differential, and both versions came equipped with Hurst shifters. The final assembly of the cars was carried out at Hurst, and owners took delivery of their cars at Hurst's Detroit facility, *not* at a Plymouth dealership.

The "not for street use" proviso allowed the hemi's underpinnings to be set up specifically for the Super/Stock 'Cudas. The rear suspension was special, and moved inboard to accommodate 7.75x15 slicks with D70x14 wide ovals up front. Bolt circles at both ends were changed from 4 to 4.5 inches to accommodate

light-weight racing wheels, and brakes were specially built by Kelsey-Hayes—with discs in front and heavy-duty drums at the rear.

Most of the creative work on the Woodward Garage project was handled by Hoover and his staff. Interestingly, one of their biggest projects was the design of the car's massive hood scoop, a legitimate piece of engineering work in its own right.

The hood scoop had as much planning as any other component on the car. Air flow characteristics were studied at length before the prototype scoop was even fabricated, and its positioning fore and aft was determined and measured as deliberately as were the height and width. The finish box served notice that what lay beneath was all business.

Inside the Woodward Garage car, things were kept to a bare minimum. Nothing remained in the stripped down cabin that wasn't necessary. In the prototype, Porsche bucket seats were pirated, but production cars were fitted with seats from the Dodge A-100 truck line. There was no back seat, but the area was carpeted for appearance. A modified Hurst "His 'n Her's" console dropped the shifter into perfect position for the driver and a dash-mounted tach head was stacked in a "can't miss" spot.

The Barracuda emblem was about all that remained untouched on this car!

The interior was stripped of every nonessential item and the stock seats replaced with buckets from a Porsche. The most important gauge was the Moroso tach, prominently mounted in the top center of the dashboard. To further reduce weight, the rear seat was removed, but rather than leave bare metal, carpeting was specially cut to cover the area.

Back in May 1968, when the first Super/Stock Hemi Barracudas were being delivered, the Woodward Garage prototype was featured in *Popular Hot Rodding* magazine. The four-page article outlined the car's development and covered Hoover's track tests at Irwindale raceway. *PHR*'s editor summed up the car's potential with one intimidating sentence: "Mustangers better watch out! This one is a real fish story from Plymouth." As it turned out, this was sage advice. The Woodward Garage project was more like a fish farm. By 1970, the Hemi 'Cuda would make the transition from Super/Stock drag car to production street car as part of the new Plymouth Rapid Transit System, the ultimate muscle car evolution of the great Chrysler 426 hemi.

WHEN THE NEEDS OF THE FEW OUTWEIGHED THE NEEDS OF THE MANY

Muscle cars were the focal point for every red-blooded American male in the mid 1970s, and even a secondhand, somewhat beat 1969 Dodge was better than anything wearing a catalytic converter and running on unleaded fuel. One day it was 426 hemi engines and 10:1 compression, the next day people were trying to figure out which Japanese cars got the best fuel economy. It was as if in one year all the fun had been siphoned out of car ownership.

Today, performance and fuel economy have managed to find middle ground, and there seems to be enough variety in the world automotive industry that anyone can find a car to suit his or her particular needs or desires. But frankly, no matter how good today's cars appear, what Chrysler did to the basic everyman's street car in the late 1960s and very early 1970s has never been duplicated. Neither the sounds, the feel, nor the look. It only happened once, and for one brief period in 1969, it happened to the Dodge Coronet.

The Dodge Scat Pack was already tearing up the road for two years before the Plymouth Rapid Transit System delivered the Hemi 'Cuda, GTX, Road Runner, Superbird, Sport Fury GT, and Duster 340, in 1970. The Dodge Super Bee 440 Six-Pack, however, was something of a midyear surprise in 1969. You could call it the tail end of the most successful ad campaign of the era, "The Dodge Rebellion," which started in 1966 with an attractive blonde actress named Pam Austin telling American men, "The Dodge Rebellion Wants You!"

It began with the Dodge Charger in 1966 and 1967, a long stretch of car with fastback styling and a 426 hemi as the top option. The original Charger body design had been considered for a production version of the Chrysler Turbine, but when the project was shelved (after 50 prototypes with a different body design were built in 1963), the sporty design seemed ideal for the 1966 Charger. It took until 1968 for Dodge stylists to fine-tune the body design, and they were dead on from 1968 to 1970 with the second-generation Charger and Charger R/T, which many consider to be the best-looking muscle car ever built in the 1960s. (Its styling has become the basis for one of Chrysler's latest concept cars, a Charger for the next century, one that might very well turn up in dealer showrooms by the early 2000s.)

The Charger is forever burned into our cinematic memories as the car Steve McQueen chased in his Mustang over the roller-coaster streets of San Francisco in the film *Bullitt*. And lest we forget the most famous Dodge Charger of all, the bright orange 01 *General Lee* from the TV series *The Dukes of Hazzard*.

In the late 1960s, Dodge was definitely in the public eye, and as it turned out, perhaps a bit too much attention was coming Dodge's way. By 1970 the insurance premiums on muscle cars were staggering. Author and photographer Randy Leffingwell noted in his 1990 book, *American Muscle*, that companies like State Farm

PAT McGRODER'S 1968 WOODWARD GARAGE HEMI 'CUDA

In the early 1990s Arizona collector Pat McGroder assembled one of the world's finest collections of rare factory prototypes, "the source cars," as he called them, for an entire generation of great American muscle machines.

"Prototypes tended to disappear, as did factory-built race cars," said McGroder. "When these cars were new they served a very specific purpose—racing—and when that was over, most were retired, and nearly all eventually wrecked and discarded. They were by nature disposable. For me, finding them is actually part of the excitement." That "excitement" often takes years and tens of thousands of dollars to fund. In the case of the 1968 Woodward Garage Hemi 'Cuda prototype, McGroder says the search for this car was one of the longest and most expensive of all.

"We were fortunate enough to have the help of Arlen Vanke, a premier race car driver for Chrysler during that time," McGroder says, "and he was able to locate the Hemi 'Cuda prototype." To ensure that the hemi was accurately restored, McGroder flew in the original Chrysler engineers who had worked on the Woodward Garage project in 1968. When they showed up on his doorstep they had all of the original design and engineering plans with them! It still took more than a year to put the car back together, matching every nut and bolt, right down to the original specifications. This is an expensive and arduous task for any restorer, when you consider that every piece of the car was literally hand-fabricated in the first place!

While it's certainly no looker, even with a 100-point restoration, it is undeniably the most significant Hemi 'Cuda of all time. A quality that only comes with being the first of its kind.

Insurance had increased rates from $500 to $800 a year in 1969 for a single male living in Los Angeles with a clean driving record. A couple of moving violations and the annual premium soared up to $2,000 a year for a Charger Daytona or Plymouth Superbird! By midyear dealers were dumping the cars for as little as $3,000.

ROAD AND TRACK

R/T stood for Road/Track, and with a 440 Magnum four-barrel V-8 under the hood, plenty of them found their way to local drag strips in the 1960s. On the pro side, Dick Landy raced two R/Ts, one with the standard 440 Magnum and another with a 426 hemi.

When Dodge announced the Scat Pack in 1968—consisting of the Coronet R/T, Charger R/T, and Dart GTS—the three cars were cleverly identified with "Bumblebee" racing stripes wrapped around the tail end instead of along the side or over the hood. Across the divisional divide, Plymouth launched its own low-buck, street/strip racer in 1968, the Belvedere-based Road Runner. Dodge was quick to counter with its own special version of the Coronet R/T, appropriately named the Super

Bee, a stripped two-door coupe with a bench front seat and minimal trim, but packing a 335-horsepower 383 V-8 and a high-performance dual exhaust system, tuned mufflers, and 2 1/4-inch tailpipes. The standard transmission was a heavy-duty four-speed with Hurst Competition-Plus floor shift. The limited option list included a TorqueFlite automatic transmission, and if you wanted to go for broke, a 426 hemi in place of the 383.

The Super Bee suspension was heavy-duty front to rear, with 0.90-inch-diameter front torsion bars, a 0.94-inch-diameter front stabilizer bar, and six rear leaf springs. The drive shaft, rear axle, and U-joints were beefed up as well. Heavy-duty shocks and drum brakes were also standard, with power front disc brakes optional.

In addition to the Bumblebee stripes, the Super Bee had its own exclusive styling trait, a power bulge in the hood with a simulated air intake. Not functional, but neat looking. The cars went on sale in February 1968 with promotional lines like, "It's the super car for the guy who doesn't want to shy away from GTOs . . . only their prices." A little over $3,000 got you on the street and the strip. The Super Bee's performance was comparable to the

From the outside, the 1969-1/2 Dodge Super Bee 440 Six-Pack was distinguished by a removable flat-black fiberglass hood, not hinged, but pinned at all four corners, and fitted with a functional air intake scoop big enough to stick your arm through. The car pictured was restored by the late Earl Dull, an avid muscle car collector who had an entire stable of Dodge and Plymouth models from the late 1960s and early 1970s. He spent more than 12 months restoring the car back in the early 1980s, and it has barely been touched since!

Under the massive fiberglass hood was the Dodge 440 Magnum V-8 equipped with three two-barrel Holley carburetors atop an Edelbrock aluminum intake manifold. Pumping out 390 horsepower and 490 lb/ft of torque, the Super Bee could peel the paint off a limit line and lay rubber all the way to 60, which took a little over 6 seconds.

Road Runner's, and factory tests turned in 0 to 60 times of 6.8 seconds with the quarter-mile covered in 15 flat.

For the Scat Pack, 1969 started out pretty much as a carryover year, with the only addition to the line-up being a hardtop version of the Super Bee coupe. Styling was virtually unchanged except for a new Bumblebee stripe design and Scat Pack medallion in the front grille and on the trunk lid. Optional simulated air scoops were available for the rear quarter panels on the Super Bee, along with a new Ramcharger fresh-air induction system identical to the Air Grabber offered on the Road Runner and GTX. The rarest of the 1969 models was the

Charger 500, specially modified by Creative Industries for NASCAR competition. The cars had flush back-lights (as opposed to the sail panels on Charger and R/T models) and were fitted with flush grilles adapted from the 1968 Dodge Coronet. The rear decklid was also redesigned and the trunk shortened. All 500 examples built were equipped with the 426 hemi, and either the TorqueFlite automatic or four-speed manual. The Charger 500 was a sell-out, and today it is a rare find.

Over at Plymouth, a new Road Runner version was rolled out for 1969 equipped with a 440 six-barrel and a removable fiberglass hood. The companion model

from Dodge came as a midyear bombshell—the down-and-dirty Super Bee 440 Six-Pack, a car that literally shouted drag strip. Like the Road Runner, it was a bad boy car in no uncertain terms, from the removable flat-black fiberglass hood—not hinged, but pinned at all four corners and fitted with a functional air intake scoop big enough to stick your arm through—to the 440 Magnum V-8 underneath. With three two-barrel Holley carburetors atop an Edelbrock aluminum intake manifold, the 440 Six-Pack could peel the paint off a limit line and lay rubber all the way to 60, which took a little over 6 seconds with the 440 pumping out 390 horsepower and 490 lb/ft of torque.

Over the years, Dodge had used all sorts of tricks to boost engine performance, but the Six-Pack was the first try at a tri-carb setup. The car's catchy name, incidentally, was created by Bob Osborn at Chrysler's advertising agency, BBD&O (Batten, Barten, Durstine & Osborn). Six-Pack was intended to imply . . . well, something intoxicating about the new Dodge.

The 440 Six-Pack came with either a four-speed manual or TorqueFlite automatic, but the real trick was how the power from the engine got to the ground. The rear end was a 9 3/4-inch Dana 60 with a 4.10:1 final drive and Sure-Grip. Taking it to the pavement were Goodyear G70X15 Polyglass tires mounted on 6-inch-wide steel wheels, painted black and bolted by chrome lug nuts.

Inside, it was as before, bare to the bones with a bench seat up front and minimal accessories, although the Super Bee had a Charger instrument panel and the midline Coronet 440 interior trim. Still, the car had only one purpose in life, to go fast, go straight, and do it from zero to 1,320 feet in the shortest possible time.

Dodge viewed 1970 as a new lease on life for the Coronet, offering the 1970 Super Bee at a new low price of $3,074 for a two-door hardtop. It was $64 less than the 1969 1/2 hardtop. Dodge called it a "triumphantly backward idea, since most performance car prices have gone up." Priced to appeal to younger buyers, the Super Bee had an extensive option list, allowing the car to be equipped with as many or as few accessories as the buyer could afford. One of the most popular was a vinyl top in black, white, green, or Gator Grain.

In its price class, the 1969 1/2 Super Bee 440 Six-Pack was one of the most formidable cars on the road. Only 271 were produced with the four-speed manual transmission and roughly 400 with TorqueFlite.

With a new decade came new body designs, and the 1970 Coronet received all-new front end sheet metal and a redesign of the rear fenderlines and taillights. Same power as the 1969 models, but not the same car.

Dodge viewed it as a new lease on life for the Coronet, offering the 1970 Super Bee at a new low price of $3,074 for a two-door hardtop. It was $64 less than the 1969 1/2 hardtop. Dodge called it a "triumphantly backward idea, since most performance car prices have gone up."

The base Super Bee came with a new three-speed fully synchronized gearbox with floor-mounted shifter (replacing the four-speed and resulting in the lower base price), fiberglass-belted wide-tread tires, and a 383 Magnum V-8. The four-speed manual from 1969 became an extra cost item added to the car's now extensive option list.

In the 1970's logos were almost as important as engines and transmissions around Chrysler corporation. Plymouth had its Road Runner, and Dodge had the Super Bee, which turned into a helmeted character on wide rubber wheels. The "bug" was boldly placed beteween the headlghts, and again at the rear of the car on the taillight trim. This beautifully restored 1970 Super Bee is owned by Tim Russell of Elton, Pennsylvania

Super Bee interiors were well designed and provided a lot of features for the money, including bucket-type front seats, center console, and wood-finish trim.

The 1970 Super Bees were easily identified by the new power bulge hood with two razor-edge, nonfunctional scoops. The words "Super Bee" appeared on the sides of the power bulge. There was also a choice of two Bumblebee striping designs, the traditional wraparound, however, now without the Bumblebee figure, or a new longitudinal stripe—two Plymouth Hemi 'Cuda "hockey sticks" forming an elongated C on the rear quarter panels. The longitudinal tape stripe came with the Bumblebee emblem, which also appeared as a badge on the taillight trim panel, and at the front of the hood between the headlamps. Another option was a rear deck spoiler, a theoretically functional wing that became an icon of the muscle car era. A new hood-mounted 8,000-rpm tachometer was also available.

Priced to appeal to younger buyers, the Super Bee had an extensive option list, allowing the car to be equipped with as many or as few accessories as the buyer could afford. Power brakes, power steering, tinted glass, front disc brakes, were all extras, as was an optional vinyl top in black, white, green, or Gator Grain. Dodge also offered five "Scat Packages" of accessories that could be installed after the car was purchased. "The Showboat" came with chromed valve covers, oil filler cap, air cleaner, hood pins and locks, and chromed road wheels. The "Read Out" included a full-sweep tachometer, oil pressure gauge, and fuel pressure gauge. "The Kruncher" offered a higher numerical ring gear and pinion, matching speedometer pinion, and Hurst shifter. The "Bee-Liever" came with a high-rise manifold and carburetor, street camshaft, and steel tubing headers. Finally, there was the "Top Eliminator" which gave Super Bee owners the otherwise discontinued 1969-style Six-Pack fiberglass hood with scoop and hood pins, Six-Pack manifold and carburetors, transistorized ignition, electric fuel pump and cool can—a coiled fuel line that could be surrounded with crushed ice—a technique which drag racers claimed could shave a tenth or so off quarter-mile times.

Heading the power options for 1970 was the 426 hemi, complete with a functional Ramcharger hood scoop (offered as an option with other engines). The 440 Six-Pack also returned for another year, although without the distinctive black fiberglass hood. Dodge reverted to the steel hood that was standard on the Super Bee.

The Super Bee was again equipped with the Rallye Suspension, a special handling package with heavy-duty torsion bars, front stabilizer, and heavy-duty rear springs, making the car more suitable to high-performance driving, albeit more in a straight line than around the decreasing radius of a hairpin curve.

Marking the beginning of a new decade, 1970 was also the beginning of the end for muscle cars. The Dodge Scat Pack found a home in "Scat City," according to the 1970 sales literature. To tell the fans all about it, Dodge formed the Scat Pack Club. You invested $3 to get a decal, patch, newsletter, and other goodies.

The Super Bee and R/T models remained the performance leaders in the Dodge stable, and 1970 versions in the hands of racer Dick Landy still did well on the stock car circuits, but this was the last year. Total sales of the Super Bee amounted to 15,506 in 1970, and the next year Coronet performance models were wiped out. Coronet coupes became Chargers, convertibles vanished, and the Super Bee survived as a Charger model for one last year.

Showing no lack of subtlety, Dodge designers offered the boldest graphics yet on the 1970 Super Bee, which covered the entire rear quarter panel.

THE REAL DAYS OF THUNDER

Designing an automobile is not easy. It requires great skill, equal amounts of patience and intuition, and above all *time*. That is what many people do not understand—the time frame in which stylists must work. Unlike most art forms which *depict* the time in which they are created, the automobile stylist must *predict* the time in which his creation will be revealed. In the case of the 1970 Plymouth Barracudas, the concept and design work had begun in 1966.

For Chrysler, the 1960s was an awkward period. Its engines were ranked among the best in the world, but its body designs were far from leading edge. Chrysler stylists were in the unenviable position of trying to catch up to their competitors at Ford and General Motors. In 1966, when the next generation Barracuda was being

The 1970 Hemi 'Cuda was powered by a 426 Hemi V-8 with two four-barrel carbs. Output was 425 horsepower.

sketched out, the Ford Mustang had already established the "pony car" concept. Chrysler also knew that Chevrolet was at work on a model to compete with the Mustang. Whatever the Dodge and Plymouth Division designers did, the niche had already been established. What they needed to do now was redefine it.

The design of the 1970 models was crucial to the future of the Barracuda. The 1967 through 1969 'Cudas had been very successful in competition, but on the showroom floor, their conservative styling was a barrier even hemi engines couldn't break. What the Plymouth design staff needed was a clean sheet of paper to work on. In 1966, they got it.

Not knowing what the Camaros would look like, it was almost a stroke of luck that the Barracudas turned out even more contemporary in design than the new Chevys. Looking at the 'Cuda's competition in 1970, the Mustang's styling was pretty aggressive, but the Camaro was a little bit softer. The design team had taken a gamble with the Barracuda, because it was a radical departure from contemporary Chrysler lines. Fortunately, Plymouth had a very active hands-on vice president of design at the time by the name of Elwood Engle, and he had some definite thoughts on the car and what it should be. "He would walk through the studio every day hollering 'Get hot!'," recalls designer John Hurlitz, now vice president of design for Daimler-Chrylser. "He'd do crazy things to get us going," says DaimlerChrysler Executive Vice President Tom Gale, who worked on the 'Cuda's engineering team in the late

1960s. "He was really wild, and I think a lot of that enthusiasm came across in what we did back then. The 'Cuda simply blew everyone away in Detroit."

It made the Mustang look old, the Camaro and Firebird tame, the GTO heavy-handed, and all the rest, the Olds 4-4-2, Chevy Chevelle, et al., just big cars with big engines. In one bold stroke, Plymouth (and Dodge) had redefined the high-performance market for the coming decade.

The long hood/short rear deck theme was even more obvious than on the Mustang, accentuated by the high trunk, short roof, and smooth, undisturbed flow of the body from bumper to bumper. This was as close as any American automaker had yet come to linear aerodynamics. The windshield wipers were recessed, door handles flush to the body, and the front end sheet metal was carried right to the leading edge, then sharply turned under. The same was done to the rear of the car. From any angle, the 'Cuda was a continual line.

The 1970 models represented as perfect a marriage of design and engineering as possible. The "Rapid Transit System" name, conceived by Jim Ramsey of Young and Rubicam, Chrysler's advertising agency, put the final touches on the entire 1970 program. The future of Dodge and Plymouth in the coming decade seemed bright and promising. And had history not taken another unexpected turn, that promise might have been fulfilled. In 1969 and 1970 Dodge and Plymouth had gone from building parental looking cars with hot engines hidden under their hoods, to building dynamic, youthful-looking cars that had engines coming through their hoods!

The RTS was made up of five basic models, 'Cuda, GTX, Sport Fury GT, Road Runner, and the Valiant Duster 340. The hot ticket items, however, were the 'Cudas and Road Runners.

The 1970 'Cuda series (apart from the stock Barracuda and Gran Coupe) offered enough options to custom tailor a car to most anyone's tastes, from a mild

The bad boy car from Dodge, the 1970 Hemi 'Cuda, was perhaps the best-styled muscle car of the entire era.

The 'Cuda's stablemate at Dodge was the Challenger R/T. Aimed at a slightly different market segment than the 'Cuda, Dodge was after the Cougar crowd, while the Plymouth version was looking to take a bite out of Mustang and Camaro Z-28 sales. The sportiest R/T model (R/T for Road/Track) was the hemi-powered convertible.

275-horsepower 340-cubic-inch V-8, to a 335-horsepower 383, 375-horsepower 440, 390-horsepower 440 six-barrel, and road-ripping 425-horsepower 426-cubic-inch hemi. The engines had equally impressive compression ratios of 10.5:1, 9.5:1, 9.7:1, 10.5:1 and 10.25:1 respectively, and an assortment of carburetors from a single Carter AVS four-barrel in the 340 and 440, to one Holley AVS four-barrel in the 383, three Holley deuces in the 440, and dual Carter AFB four-barrel carbs in the hemi.

The 1970 Plymouth models could leave a trail of burnt rubber behind every shift, delivering their 340, 425, 480, and breathtaking 490 lb/ft of respective torque. The power was carried through Heavy-Duty three- or four-speed manuals in 340 and 383 models, and a Heavy-Duty four-speed with Hurst linkage in the

440 and hemi cars. A high-upshift TorqueFlite automatic with "Slap Stick" shifter was optional on the 340 and 383, standard on the others.

Filling out the order sheet on a 'Cuda was like ordering off a Chinese menu. On 'Cudas with the 340 or 383 engines and three-speed or optional four-speed, a 3.23:1 axle ratio was standard. Rear ends for the 440 and hemi were extra heavy-duty Dana 60 axles with a 9 3/4-inch ring gear. Available with the four-speed Performance Axle Package were 3.55:1 or 3.91:1 ratios. Larger displacement engines offered 3.54:1 with the four-speed stick, or a 4.10:1 optional. With the TorqueFlite, 3.23:1 was standard, and a 3.55:1 or 4.10:1 ratio was optional as part of the Performance Axle Package, which included a Sure-Grip differential. And with six you got egg rolls.

Pushing the performance limits even further, the 'Cuda series offered suspensions specially tuned for the output of each car. The high-performance 440s and hemis were equipped with extra heavy-duty torsion bars (0.92-inch diameter) and stabilizer bars (0.94-inch diameter) up front and extra heavy-duty shocks all around. Rear suspensions used extra heavy-duty five-leaf plus two half-leaf springs on the left, and extra heavy-duty six-leaf springs on the right. The two extra half leaves on the left were to prevent torque steer off the line with the larger engines!

To bring all this horsepower to a stop, Plymouth provided 11x3-inch self adjusting cast iron drums, or

optional full floating caliper disc brakes up front and 11x2 1/2-inch drums for the rear.

On the Hemi 'Cuda, rims were 15x7 with F60x15 tires standard. The 440s were shod with 14x6 rims and F70x14 rubber, as was the 383. The more streetable 340 used the hemi's 15-inch rims but with E60x15 tires.

With plenty of competitive muscle, the 'Cuda series showed it off with an array of color schemes that could turn heads a block away. Along the side of the cars was an inverted "hockey stick" flat-black paint stripe that started above the door handles, followed the fenderline toward the rear, and turned down at the back. Lettered inside the head of the "stick" was either the word

From the rear there was a definite similarity between the 'Cuda and Challenger, which shared nearly identical sheet metal.

There was no mistaking a Plymouth Superbird, the winged wonder with the Road Runner emblem prominently displayed. This pretty much cast the rest of the muscle car crowd as Wile E. Coyote. Under the hood of this bright yellow Bird is the popular 390-horsepower 440 six-barrel.

"HEMI" or the numbers "340", "383", or "440", depending upon the engine. The real eye-catcher, however, was up front, the Hemi 'Cuda's Shaker air scoop protruding through a cutout in the hood. The sides of the scoop had bold lettering that read "Hemicuda." A Chrysler guy once said that was so Mustang and Camaro owners could know exactly what kind of car it was that blew them off!

Among the options offered on the 'Cuda series were "Elastomeric" front and rear bumpers, which were the stock unchromed bumpers covered with body color–keyed urethane. Two packages were available, one with the front bumper in any of nine body colors with matching racing mirrors, the other with front and rear bumpers and mir-

rors in Rallye Red. Other options included a rear spoiler, and rear window louvers with black vinyl roof, blackout moldings, and color-keyed racing mirrors.

Only 652 Hemi 'Cudas were built in 1970, 284 with four-speeds and 368 with TorqueFlite. The 1971 hemi models were to be the last flat out, no respect for noise or fuel economy high-performance cars. In 1972 the 426 hemi, 440 Six-Pack, and 383 were gone.

ROAD RUNNER AND SUPERBIRD . . . BEEP-BEEP!

The 1970 'Cudas ran with some pretty fast company. Among the five models that made up the Rapid Transit System were the limited production NASCAR-based

Said Chrysler-Plymouth in 1970: "The Road Runner SuperBird is a study in ultra-high speed aerodynamics. The aerodynamic nose cone is 19 inches long and stretches the over-all length of the limited edition Road Runner to 221 inches—17.2 inches longer than the standard Road Runner's 203.8 inch length. The rear stabilizer is mounted 25 inches above the rear deck."

Superbirds. Described by Plymouth as "the ultimate Road Runner," only 2,000 were built.

Along with the Dodge Charger 500, the Superbird and its winged counterpart, the Dodge Charger Daytona, were all produced for Chrysler Corporation by Creative Industries, which handled the special assembly of the cars. While basically Road Runners at heart, the Superbirds had enough modifications to the standard body to make normal assembly line manufacturing impractical. Special front and rear designs to improve aerodynamics at high speeds, and a specially molded convex rear window were added to the Road Runner body.

Sometimes sheet metal comes from strange places. Such was the case with the Road Runner. In order to attach the Superbird's extended front nose cone and concealed pop-up headlights, 1970 Dodge Coronet front fenders were used on Superbirds! The cars also required a good deal of special exterior work. Under the skin and inside, however, they were Road Runners with the same engines, drivetrains, and suspension options used throughout the RTS, though Superbirds offered more standard equipment.

The specific production number of 2,000 cars was established to homologate the Superbird as a production car, according to NASCAR rules. In race trim, the long-nosed, high-tailed 1970 Road Runners racked up eight NASCAR Grand National victories—five with Richard Petty behind the wheel. Impressive, but not enough to win the season. The Grand National title, however, was not far from home, having gone to Bobby Isaac and the

A bright yellow Superbird was a speeding ticket waiting to happen, and insurance companies zeroed in on the big Plymouths driving premiums up even for good drivers. By the end of 1970, dealers were dumping the cars because most people couldn't afford the insurance, especially on models equipped with the 390-horsepower 440 Six Pack.

The Superbird's counterpart was the Dodge Charger Daytona, which took the 1970 Grand National with Bobby Isaac behind the wheel. With the Daytona, Isaac set a closed-course speed record of 201.104 miles per hour, which would remain unbroken for the next 13 years!

On the track in 1969, the Dodge Daytonas made an impressive first year showing. Their immediate popularity helped Chrysler make the decision to offer a Plymouth version in 1970.

Superbird look-a-like Dodge Charger Daytona. Isaac set a closed-course speed record of 201.104 miles per hour, which would remain unbroken for the next 13 years!

Built for only one year (Chrysler planned to withdraw from NASCAR competition in 1971), the Superbird became the flagship of the Rapid Transit System, and street versions, limited in numbers as they were, still came with a full array of options and three different engine choices. Standard was the 375-horsepower 440-cubic-inch four-barrel V-8, with optional 390-horsepower six-barrel 440, or the 425-horsepower 426-cubic-inch dual four-barrel hemi. For transmissions, there were two available, the TorqueFlite automatic which included the Performance Axle Package, or the four-speed manual with the Trak Pack. Rear axle ratios offered were 3.54:1 standard, 4.10:1 optional with the four-speed, and 3.23:1 standard, 3.55:1 and 4.10:1 optional with the TorqueFlite. The Birds rode on F70x14 Goodyear wide-profile tires wrapped around rallye wheels.

Standard features on the cars included power steering, power front disc brakes, and a distinctive vinyl roof. The only options aside from engine/trans selections were bucket seats, F60x15 Goodyear extrawide tires, and the usual sound system upgrades. Customers could also choose from seven exterior colors—Alpine White, Vitamin C Orange, Lemon Twist, Lime Light, Fire Metallic, Tor-Red, and Corporation Blue.

While the Superbird and Charger Daytona appeared to be the same car, there were some dividing lines that set the Plymouth and Dodge models apart. The nose cones were not interchangeable, for example, nor were the rear wings. The rear uprights supporting the horizontal stabilizer were unique to the Superbird, being slightly more swept back than those of the Daytona.

Street versions came with a 150-mile-per-hour speedometer (tachometer was optional), and cars equipped with the 426 hemi could use up every numeral on the dial! Even the 440 six-barrel–powered Superbirds were capable of 140 miles per hour. On either the track or the street, the Plymouth Superbirds were cars to be reckoned with.

Less dramatic in appearance, but produced in far greater numbers, were the standard Road Runners, which in their own right dominated local drag strips across the country. The Road Runner model was already well established before the Rapid Transit System was introduced, having won *Motor Trend*'s "Car of the Year" award in 1969.

The high-winged Daytona was similar to the Superbird, but the rear stabilizer was of a different design and angle than the Plymouth's.

Big Dodge Magnum V-8 gave the Daytona street cars plenty of competitive power.

From any angle, the Dodge Challenger T/A was a mean piece of work.

For 1970, the car was reskinned with new front and rear end designs, a mock air scoop forward of the rear wheels, and a new hood sporting a raised center section or "power bulge." The Road Runner was offered in three models—not counting the Superbird—a two-door coupe, two-door hardtop, and the most stylish of the three, a two-door convertible.

Base engine was a 335-horsepower 383-cubic-inch V-8 with Holley four-barrel. Optional engines were the 440 six-barrel and 426 hemi. Standard output from the 440 six-barrel was 375 horsepower in the Road Runner paired with a heavy-duty three-speed floor shifter. As an option, either a heavy-duty four-speed or TorqueFlite automatic could be ordered.

Cars running the 440 had a slick little "visual aid" that Plymouth dubbed the "Air Grabber." An electronic solenoid switch inside the car operated a vacuum-activated hood scoop which raised up menacingly from the center of the power bulge. More than mild intimidation when accompanied by a well-revved engine! The Air

Grabber was standard equipment on hemi-equipped cars, but not available on the Superbird.

The Road Runners (and GTX) had their own list of power options and gear ratios. Standard with either the TorqueFlite, or the three-speed or four-speed manual was a 3.23:1 axle ratio. Options were a 3.55:1 or 3.91:1, both with a Sure-Grip differential. With the 440 or hemi the 3.23:1 was standard with TorqueFlite, and a 3.55:1 with Sure-Grip was optional. The four-speed came with a 3.54:1 and Sure-Grip. Optional for both automatic and manual transmissions was the high-torque 4.10:1 ratio with Sure-Grip. As with the 440 six-barrel and 426 Hemi 'Cuda, Road Runners equipped with these engines also had the heavy-duty Dana 60 rear end and heavy-duty suspensions.

On the options list, along with the usual radio and dealer-equipped add-ons, Road Runner purchasers had the choice of new contoured bucket seats, a vinyl roof, flat-black hood striping over the power bulge, Road Runner "bird" decals, and a total of 18 different exterior colors!

The AAR 'Cuda, like this one from the Tim Callihan collection, was the wildest looking and best handling 'Cuda produced. It was only offered in 1970 and was powered by a 340-cubic-inch V-8 with three Holly two-barrel carbs on an Edelbrock aluminum intake manifold. The same engine was used in the companion Dodge Challenger T/A, but was not available on any other Dodge or Plymouth model.

THE CHALLENGER T/A AND AAR 'CUDA

Aside from the Daytona, there was the Challenger T/A, Dodge's spinoff of the hot Plymouth AAR 'Cuda. Built for only one year, the Challenger T/A was limited to 2,539 cars aimed directly at the Camaro Z28, Firebird Trans Am, and Mustang market. The cars were hardline competition models, offered with only one engine, a 340-cubic-inch Six-Pack V-8 rated at 290 horsepower. These engines were built specifically for the Challenger T/A (and Plymouth AAR 'Cuda), and had reinforced main bearing webs, specially machined cylinder heads, and had the pushrod holes relocated to allow for larger ports. Longer than normal pushrods were used with special ends for rocker arm adjusting screws. The lifters were hydraulic with heavy-duty snap rings, and the rocker shafts had additional lube spreader grooves. Cylinder

137

blocks in Challenger T/As were specially numbered and had the letters *TA* included in the cast-in serial number.

The high-performance V-8 exhaled via a low restriction, dual exhaust system with two-pass mufflers emerging through belled tubes under the side sills just forward of the rear wheel openings.

Power was delivered through a close-ratio four-speed built specifically for the T/A and AAR 'Cudas. First was 2.74:1, second 1.77:1, third 1.34:1, and fourth 1:1. As an option, the Torque-Flite automatic transmission was also available.

Special front fenders had to be made for the Challenger T/As and AAR 'Cudas to cover the stock steel 15x7-inch wheels and fat G60x15 rear and E60x15 front tires. Also specific to these cars was an increased rear spring camber to provide ground clearance for the special side outlet exhausts and larger rear tires.

The list of standard features included a special Rallye Suspension with front and rear sway bars, heavy-duty shocks, power front disc brakes and 11-inch rear drums, and a rear deck lid spoiler. Options included power-assisted steering, a front spoiler, and a

In 1970, Chrysler Corporation put another performance notch in its belt with the most legendary American muscle cars of the era, the Plymouth AAR and Hemi 'Cuda, the Road Runner, Superbird, Dodge Daytona, and Challenger. These were cars that truly defined Chrysler's adaptability to changing trends. The 'Cuda became one of the most significant American cars of the era, and the last of the great Chrysler Corporation muscle cars. From front to rear, the Dodge Challenger T/A, Plymouth 426 Hemi 'Cuda, 383 Road Runner and Superbird.

Another popular Plymouth muscle car for 1970 was the two-door hardtop GTX, part of the new Rapid Transit System.

The top-of-the-line Plymouth for 1970 was the luxurious Sport Fury. Two versions were offered, the sporty S-23 and high-performance Sport Fury GT.

The 1971 Hemi 'Cudas were the last flat-out performance models. This one is rare, even among 'Cudas, a convertible equipped with the 425-horsepower 426 hemi, Shaker air scoop, and heavy-duty Hurst four-speed gearbox. Only a handful were ordered in this configuration, and 1971 marked the last year for the 'Cuda convertible.

Equipped with the 426 hemi and Shaker hood, the 'Cuda was one stunning automobile. Even a generation later, people stop and look when a restored hemi car drives by.

It was the beginning of the end for muscle cars in 1971, and Plymouth was headed down the road with a last best effort to put performance in the hands of motoring enthusiasts.

A well appointed interior made the Hemi 'Cuda one of the most attractive and comfortable muscle cars of the era.

The Scat Pack offered cars in every size, shape, and price. The Dodge Coronet Super Bee was the counterpart to the Plymouth Road Runner. The sportiest Dodge (except for the limited edition Charger Daytona) was the Challenger R/T, available in coupe and convertible. For those on a budget but performance minded, Dodge had the affordable Dart Swinger. The heavy hitter was the very stylish Dodge Charger R/T. An R/T version was also available on the lower-priced Dodge Coronet.

fiberglass hood with functional air scoop. What came at no extra cost was sheer power—0 to 60 in 5.8 seconds, to 100 miles per hour in 14.4, and through the quarter in 14.3 at 99.5 miles per hour. The 1970 Challenger T/A was worthy of great expletives, but most people were simply speechless!

For Plymouth, 1970 was a pretty good year, and for muscle car and pony car enthusiasts it was a great year. The Rapid Transit System put some of Chrysler's best ever performance cars on the road. Competition from across town, at American Motors, had a few heads turning with Mark Donohue behind the wheel of AMC's Trans-Am Javelin. Street versions of the race car painted in red, white, and blue were packing a 390-cubic-inch V-8, Ram Air, and a four-speed with Hurst shifter. Behind that, AMC had the redesigned Javelin AMX. Ford offered the Mustang Mach 1, Boss 302, and 429 Cobra Jet Shelby. Mercury had the 300-horse-power Cougar Eliminator, while General Motors had the Camaro Z28 and Firebird Trans Am.

The greatest competition of all, however, was to come in the following three years from the federal government, OPEC, and the nation's insurance companies. A triumvirate not even Hemi 'Cudas, Shelby Mustangs, and Z28 Camaros could overcome.

By the early 1970s that old economic demon was back. There was a recession and political tension, and the tastes of American automotive consumers were jolted from performance and cubic inches to economy and liters—the fewer the better. The convertible was gone, gas guzzlers were on the resale lot, and folks were finding out that Honda built more than motorcycles. People weren't sitting in line at the local drag strip to get a timing slip, but were waiting in line at the local gas station to fill their tanks. Somewhere in all this confusion, the muscle car era came to an end.

Plymouth had a comparable model to the affordable Dodge Swinger, the Duster 340, which put a high-performance 340-cubic-inch V-8 under the hood of a Plymouth compact car.

143

The bust that should have boomed. In 1981 Chrysler revived the Imperial name and attached it to a strikingly designed two-door luxury car. Lee Iacocca appeared in ads saying, "Our new Imperial is an electronic marvel." Handsomely styled in the Cordoba profile, accented with a bold grille, concealed headlights, and a fastback sail panel of classic proportions, the Imperial should have been a smashing success. It wasn't. In 1981 only 7,225 were sold. In 1982, when this Frank Sinatra Edition was introduced in blue, 2,329 sold, including 279 Sinatra models. "And now, the end is near. . . . "

in the face of a turbulent 1975 model year, Chrysler's market share fell to a low of 14 percent, half that of Ford, and almost insignificant compared to GM's commanding 53 percent share of new car sales.

With the half-way point of the decade behind it, Chrysler joined the rest of the new car industry in rebounding sales throughout 1976 and 1977. Chrysler Corporation continued to downsize its cars and expand the imports, adding the Mitsubishi-built Plymouth Arrow to the model line. Cordoba was still Chrysler's best-selling model, and the new 1976 Aspen and Volaré compacts were winners for Dodge and Plymouth. It seemed for the moment that the worst was over. It was, unfortunately, the calm before the storm.

In 1977 Chrysler Corporation increased its production by 25 percent with Cordoba outselling other Chrysler makes by better than two to one. Both Plymouth and Dodge passed the half-million mark, with the divisions taking sixth and seventh place, respectively, in new cars, thanks in part to delivering more than 118,000 imported Colts and Arrows.

Having done its homework for the better part of the decade, Chrysler became the first American auto maker to build a domestic, front-wheel drive subcompact car,

Lee Iacocca went raiding in the early 1980s, and he pulled Ford's most famous namesake from Dearborn, enlisting the aid of Carroll Shelby to brand his name on a new, sporty Dodge, the 1984 Shelby Charger.

This was Chrysler's turnaround year with the Shelby, the introduction of the Dodge and Plymouth minivans, and a LeBaron Town & Country wood-sided convertible (introduced midyear in 1983), to capitalize on the company's legendary 1946–1948 woody convertibles. The new models featured simulated white ash framework and mahogany inserts, and sported Mark Cross designer leather bucket seats.

introducing the Omni and Horizon in 1978. Powered by imported VW four-cylinder engines, the styling of both cars was patterned after the successful Volkswagen Rabbit. Chrysler executives had hoped Omni and Horizon would be the magic pill. They weren't. Consumers were slow to warm to the new little Dodge and Plymouth models, and Chrysler's market share slipped. The headlines in the November 2 issue of the *Detroit Free Press* said it all—"Chrysler Losses Are Worst Ever."

The new LeBaron line introduced in 1977 had bumped the Cordoba from the top of the Chrysler best-seller list by 1978, and now there were four imports in the Pentastar fold, Dodge Colt, Dodge Challenger, Plymouth Arrow, and Plymouth Sapporo, all manufactured by Mitsubishi.

Chrysler made another heroic effort to give customers what they wanted with the launch of the 1979 models in the fall of 1978. Omni and Horizon sales picked up with the addition of two sporty hatchback coupes, the Dodge 024 and Plymouth TC3. The LeBaron line was making headway with new Town & Country versions of the station wagon, and an attempt to revive the Chrysler 300 name was tried on a special version of the Cordoba. Ironically, just when Chrysler finally had some decent small cars, Americans decided they wanted big cars again.

As the new model year followed the calendar into 1979, sales were starting to pick up. Then the second oil crisis hit in the spring, and the economy went into free fall. Compounded by double-digit inflation, high interest rates, and the promise of higher prices at the pump, new car sales plunged once more, and Chrysler started to hemorrhage red ink—$1.1 billion worth.

The Iacocca/Shelby formula of the 1960s still worked in the 1980s, only now it was for Chrysler. In 1988 they teamed up again to produce the CSX. The Shelby CSX was the same idea as the old Mustang GT 350. "Take a good car and make it goodern," to quote Shelby. The school of thought for the CSX was somewhat different than the build-a-bigger-motor days of the 1960s. In 1980s thinking, bigger wasn't better, because a turbocharged, intercooled four could kick dust in the face of a normally aspirated V-8. Shelby modified the engine to squeeze every ounce of power, improved the suspension, added a few custom touches, and the Dodge Shadow became a 175-horsepower, 125-mile-per-hour CSX. Shelby's own 15x6 Centurion light-alloy wheels wearing Goodyear Eagle Gatorback VR 205/50VR15 tires, completed the package. Color choices? One. Black and gray. The price? A reasonable $14,160.

In 1987 Chrysler introduced a sporty new LeBaron coupe and convertible and a sneak peak at a forthcoming Chrysler Maserati sports car. It took two years for Chrysler and DeTomaso in Italy to get the TC into production, by which time the sleek LeBarons, upon which the Maserati's body styling was based, had become so popular that the Maserati TC was barely distinguishable. In fact, the LeBaron, with its hidden headlights, was actually better looking. At $30,000, the Chrysler Maserati TC sold poorly and was dropped in 1990, after only 7,500 were built.

THE LEE IACOCCA YEARS

Given the condition Chrysler was in by the end of the 1970s, it is remarkable—no, make that astonishing—that the company could have come out with as strong a model line as it did in 1980, spearheaded by an all-new Cordoba, a car that will likely go down in the history books as one of the best-looking American automobiles of its time.

Chrysler had finally pulled together a line-up of cars that had eye appeal, price, and respectable fuel economy, and had it been any year other than 1980, sales probably would have been admirable. It was an election year, the economy was still struggling, the stock market was waffling at 700, and President Jimmy Carter was mired in a political crisis with Iran, the U.S. Embassy hostages, and a disastrously failed rescue attempt. By year's end Carter was out of a job, the auto industry was out of luck, and Chrysler had blown through $800 million dollars of federal loans, against a ledger sheet running red with $1.7 billion in losses. Chrysler's new boss, Lee A. Iacocca, had engineered the federal bailout loans to keep Chrysler from going bankrupt in 1979, and putting a good percentage of the auto industry's blue collar workers (around 800,000) on the unemployment roles, something the Carter administration did not need.

Lee Iacocca was already a legend in Detroit automotive circles when he joined Chrysler in November 1978; he was the father of the Mustang, former president of Ford Motor Company, and the man who had stood on the wrong side of Henry Ford II's desk one too many times on June 13, 1978, when "Hank the Deuce" fired his number two man.

HELL HATH NO FURY LIKE AN IACOCCA SCORNED

As soon as he arrived at Chrysler, Lee Iacocca raided Ford Motor Company management, recruiting a handful of top executives, including Gerald Greenwald (who became Chrysler Corporation chairman in 1985), Steve Miller (who would be instrumental in securing the federal loan guarantees in 1979), and Gar Laux, who had been sales manager of the Ford Division when the Mustang was introduced in 1964. Product planner Hal Sperlich had already gone to Chrysler in 1978, having been given the boot by Henry Ford II in 1977. How ironic for Ford. It was Sperlich's concept of the K-car that would save Chrysler in the 1980s.

With his team in place, Iacocca appealed to Congress for loan guarantees that would allow Chrysler to stay in business and build a new line of cars. After requesting and receiving concessions from the UAW, renegotiating outstanding loans, and convincing the powers that be on Capital Hill that every penny borrowed would be repaid (the government essentially cosigned Chrysler's loans), a credit line of $1.5 billion was issued.

THE NEW CHRYSLER CORPORATION

Lee Iacocca started an advertising trend in the 1980s, which to this day is still practiced. When the chairman and CEO of a company shows his face on television commercials and in print ads, people begin to see an individual rather than a company. If they happen to like that individual (which they did, making Iacocca the most recognized corporate executive in history) and believe in him (which the public did) then the public also believes in the product. It worked for Iacocca and

Chrysler, and fortunately, by the early 1980s there were products behind Iacocca worth believing in.

The front-wheel drive K-car platform, launched in 1981 as the Plymouth Reliant and Dodge Aries, worked its way into the Chrysler line by 1982 as the all-new LeBaron and Dodge 400. Engineering had essentially stretched the K-cars' wheelbase to accommodate larger body styles, and the formula continued to work throughout the decade, as did the LeBaron name, which attracted buyers to a variety of body styles from sedans and coupes to sporty convertibles. (Chrysler was the first American auto maker to resurrect the rag top with the 1982 LeBaron and Dodge 400 models.)

The K-car concept and K-car derivatives gave Chrysler one of the best-selling product lines in America. In what was one of the biggest media events in automotive history, in 1983 Lee Iacocca presented a check for almost $1 billion, to pay off the bulk of Chrysler's loans, seven years before they were due! By the end of the year, all $1.2 billion in federally guaranteed loans had been repaid. Chrysler was in the black.

CHRYSLER'S MAGIC WAGON

ENTER THE GARAGEABLE MINI-VAN

The minivan was not a new idea, at least in Europe and Japan, where small, garageable vans had been on the road since the late 1960s. The Japanese really were the first to make practical (for Japan) compact vans.

In the mid-1970s, Nissan, Toyota, and Mitsubishi were the world leaders in compact van technology, with models like the Nissan Caravan, Toyota Hiace, and Mitsubishi Delcia. Toyota built the first minivan in 1967, but Japanese vans were never exported to this country until after Chrysler introduced the Dodge Caravan in 1983.

The Japanese had been reluctant to export minivans because of Detroit's escalating pressure on Congress to write legislation that would restrict the number of imported cars. By the late 1970s, Japan, Inc., was carving up domestic auto sales with Toyota, Datsun (Nissan), and Honda dealerships springing up from coast to coast. The minivans, however, were never really considered practical for the U.S. market.

The idea of a small, garageable van had been discussed for years, but Chrysler was the first to act on it. The 1983 prototype set the standard for an entire generation of new family vehicles.

The only imported small van that made any inroads with Americans was the hippie icon of the 1960s and 1970s, the VW bus. Americans were otherwise knee-deep in an era of full-sized vans built for tradesmen, or customized as rolling bedrooms for a pop culture of vanners whose numbers had grown to nearly equal those of hot rodders and low riders by the late 1970s.

Interestingly, most of the features that would eventually come to pass on American minivans, including folding rear seats and driver- and passenger-side sliding doors, had been *de rigueur* on Japanese vans like the Toyota Hiace, since 1977.

In 1983 Chrysler created a new niche market with the Dodge and Plymouth minivans. Its "magic wagon" would go on to virtually replace the station wagon, revolutionize the cup holder industry (which began with custom vans in the 1970s), put a family room on wheels, and forever change the landscape of our highways.

Many industry pundits predicted that the magic wagon's final trick would be that of disappearing, but with industry sales in the late 1990s averaging 1.2 million, the minivan appears to have become a staple of American motoring life.

Since creating the market segment, Chrysler has continually been the leader in the field, being the first to introduce a driver-side sliding door, standard driver air bag, standard passenger air bag, integrated child safety seats, and cab-forward design.

"In order to dominate a market segment for more than 15 years, it's critical to constantly refine the product or expand upon it," says James P. Holden, Chrysler's executive vice president of sales and marketing, and general manager of minivan operations. "By offering industry firsts, we are able to keep our minivans top-of-mind with potential buyers. And by offering minivans like the latest Town & Country Limited, the ultimate luxury minivan, we are able to grow the market by creating segments within the market."

Over the past half-century, each decade has produced one or more memorable vehicles—not necessarily classics, but vehicles that contributed to the social fabric of their time. They include the Volkswagen Beetle, the Chevrolet Corvette, 1955 Ford Thunderbird, the 1965 Ford Mustang, and certainly, the Dodge, Plymouth and Chrysler Town & Country minivans, which started a cultural revolution within the American automotive industry. Since 1983 Chrysler Corporation has sold more than seven million minivans.

When the hourglass ran out on the 1980s, Chrysler Corporation had rebuilt itself into an empire, launching the Dodge Caravan and Plymouth Voyager minivans in 1984, acquiring American Motors (to get Jeep) in 1987, purchasing Lamborghini outright, and establishing a partnership with Mitsubishi in 1988. The ebb and flow of the industry took Chrysler on a few joy rides during the decade, and by 1988 sales had begun to slip once more, with the K-car and its endless variations having grown a bit long in the tooth. The downturn, however, was only temporary, for in the wings a new generation of Chryslers was being developed for the 1990s under the direction of new Executive Vice President Robert Lutz, and Chrysler's new vice president of design, Thomas C. Gale.

Bob Lutz brought years of experience with him when he joined Chrysler in June 1986. He had worked for General Motors in Europe, spent three years with BMW, and then joined Ford Motor Company as chairman of Ford of Europe, executive vice president of international operations, and finally executive vice president of truck operations. Tom Gale had spent his entire career with Chrysler, starting with the design team that created the benchmark 1970 Plymouth Hemi 'Cuda. Together their vision would forge a new generation of Chrysler, Dodge, and Plymouth products for the decade to come. In 1989 the first real evidence of that vision appeared at the Detroit and Los Angeles auto shows. It was a concept car called the Viper RT/10.

For Chrysler, the 1990s were to be the best years in the company's history.

Over the years, the Chrysler design studio refined the shape and the features of the minivan several times, finally adding a driver-side sliding door and cab-forward styling to the latest version.

CHAPTER 10

TOM GALE AND THE CHRYSLER DESIGN STAFF

The men who put Chrysler styling back on top

Thomas C. Gale is executive vice president, Chrysler product development, design, and passenger car operations, and some say, the man whose vision of Chrysler's future in the mid-1980s helped create the Chrysler Corporation of the 1990s.

Gale began his career with Chrysler more than 30 years ago, in December 1967. "It was just after grad school and I was offered an engineering position at Chrysler." He stops to reflect on the irony. "I was trained as a designer, but I spent my first four years at Chrysler in engineering! I was in the door, though, and I figured I could never go from design to engineering, but I could go from engineering to design."

Tom Gale's first assignment with Chrysler was the Plymouth Barracuda. "I've always wanted an AAR 'Cuda," says Gale, pictured with the 1999 Dodge Power Wagon concept truck. "It's like *déjà vu*, you take it apart and all the belt and belt weather strips, and body and body structures, all of the things you designed 30 years ago are there."

The body design of the Portofino was far more revealing of future Chrysler design than most realized. A lot of the cab-forward styling seen on current models like the Dodge Intrepid and Chrysler LHS are evident in the Portofino's profile and rear view. Unlike the production cars, the Lamborghini had four rotational doors that opened upward and a V-8 engine placed forward of the rear axle. *Dennis Adler*

Hurlitz spearheaded two of the company's most successful muscle cars, the 1970 Plymouth Hemi 'Cuda and AAR 'Cuda.

For Gale, Hurlitz, and Walling, among others within Chrysler, 1970 was the beginning of a crusade to push the limits of contemporary styling, but that journey was to have many, many detours. Throughout the next three decades, they endeavored to give Chrysler cutting edge designs. Unfortunately, what the design teams envisioned, and what Chrysler management in the 1970s and 1980s could afford, more often were two different things. "John, Neil and I really wanted to try and change the company, to do something a little different, but it wasn't easy," says Gale.

In the early 1970s, it was a difficult task. The muscle car era had fizzled in the wake of government regulations, gas shortages, and a roller coaster economy. "All of the events of the 1970s conspired against Chrysler in some respects," recalls Gale. "We weren't always the healthiest financially. And then you had to deal with all the new regulations, had to worry a little bit about what they would do to competitiveness. I'm not complaining about regulations, I think regulations are fine, and everybody has to

His first assignment under Chrysler chief stylist Elwood Engel was the engineering for the 1970 Plymouth Barracuda and Hemi 'Cuda. Working on the Barracuda's body styling was another young designer named John Hurlitz, who has been Gale's associate now for more than 30 years, and is currently vice president of design for DaimlerChrylser.

Along with stylist Neil Walling, who retired in 1999 as vice president of advanced design, Gale and

At just 168.8 inches, the Pronto and Pronto Cruiser concept vehicles' overall length is 5.3 inches shorter than the new Ford Focus, yet the interior volume of 119.8 cubic feet rivals that of a full-sized sedan. The PT Cruiser may be the first instance of niche marketing creating the niche!

deal with them, but sometimes regulations affect various competitors in different ways. This has always been the case with Chrysler, and in the 1970s, whether it was fuel economy, or emissions, they took away things and made it difficult to recoup investments."

The other predicament that slowed Chrysler in the 1970s was the new Corporate Average Fuel Economy (CAFE). Automakers had to meet a predetermined average fuel economy for the entire company. It didn't matter to the fed how you got there, just so long as you arrived. Big cars with poor mileage had to be offset by fuel-efficient economy cars. That was one of the leading causes of the muscle car's demise. The price of gasoline was another. Oil had become an international bargaining chip. OPEC (Organization of Petroleum Exporting Countries) suddenly became a world power in 1973, and oil companies began raising their prices. By the mid-1970s, after

Just a few short years ago the Plymouth Prowler, shown here as a concept vehicle, was an auto show teaser . . .

. . . and today it is one of Chrysler's sportiest production cars. The original purple color has been joined by black, yellow, red, and for 2000, silver.

Arguably the most dynamic concept vehicle to come from Chrysler in the 1990s was the 1998 Chronos. The stunning combination of futuristic and retro styling perfectly captured the essence of the legendary Virgil Exner–designed Chrysler Ghias of the early 1950s, seamlessly integrated with contemporary aerodynamics. If we could beg for one concept car to go into production for the twenty-first century, this would be the one.

From concept to reality, the Viper went from auto show to showroom in record time. The introduction came in 1993, the same year as Chrysler's debut of cab-forward styling on the Concorde, Intrepid, and (Jeep Division) Eagle Vision. It was a remarkable year for Chrysler.

DaimlerChrysler's new headquarters in Auburn Hills, Michigan, is the most modern automotive design, engineering, and production center in the world. In October 1999, the Chrysler Technical Center opened the Walter P. Chrysler Museum on the CTC grounds as an educational center open to the public.

price hikes at the pump, rationing and gas lines, consumers were far more interested in miles per gallon than miles per hour. Automakers had to rethink horsepower, performance, chassis design, weight, the cost of catalytic converters, and the effects on engines of lower octane ratings and unleaded fuel. Design and engineering suddenly became a series of tradeoffs; you give up one thing to gain another, less performance for better economy, facelifted body designs instead of all-new designs in order to recoup the costs of new engineering. It was not exactly the best environment for creative thinking. "That," says Gale with emphasis, "dramatically affected our ability to do the next generation of Chrysler products in the 1970s. Meeting regulations was really a double whammy, and most people don't understand that side of design and engineering."

All of Detroit's automakers were caught up in the same predicament, but Chrysler was faring worse than GM or Ford. Chrysler had a few hits in the late 1970s, like the Cordoba, Dodge Aspen, and Plymouth Volare, but it would take more than a decade and a federal bailout before Chrysler could rebound.

For almost two decades, performance had been a topic whispered about in small circles of motoring enthusiasts and in the advanced styling and engineering departments of Detroit's automakers. The road back was a long one while designers and engineers developed a new generation of safer, better-built, and more fuel-efficient cars that would emerge in the late 1980s and early 1990s. Between 1973 and 1993, the American automotive industry, and the American consumer, saw more technological breakthroughs than at any time in the last half-century.

STYLING THE NEW CHRYSLER CORPORATION

"The market place reacts by doing different things. This led to the birth of sport utility vehicles, minivans, sport trucks, and personal use trucks, vehicles that were really just disguised luxury vehicles and passenger cars. Fortunately, when I took over design in 1985, I think we prioritized the right things. We went after minivans, we went after sport utilities, we went after trucks, and doing things that really took us toward being a different company," says Gale.

By the late 1980s, Chrysler had rebuilt itself with stylish new cars, not yet trend-setting cars, but Gale's design staff was making inroads with models like the sporty LeBaron convertible, and show cars like the 1987 Portofino.

A collaboration between Chrysler design staff and Lamborghini (at the time owned by Chrysler), the Portofino introduced the cab-forward look that would appear on Chrysler concept cars in the early 1990s and characterize the all-new 1993 Chrysler and Dodge models. Since 1993, Chrysler design has never looked back. Chrysler concept cars set new standards for research and development in the 1990s. They were more than auto show exhibits to wow the public with "what might be," but were an unveiling of "what would be."

"I've always believed that good design adds value faster than it adds cost," says Gale. "But first I had to spend years just building credibility. You have to gain the confidence of management that you're not going to do something crazy" (Gale takes a breath as if to field the question before it is even asked) "and Viper wasn't crazy—it was done for image, to put a face on all Dodge products. Those kinds of icons are important."

Building an image for Chrysler, Dodge, and Plymouth was one of Gale's top priorities, and he accomplished it to a

Although Chrysler has owned Jeep since 1987, the Dodge Division had been a leader in sport truck design for years and at one time had built the great Dodge Ramcharger sport utility. In 1998 Dodge took its "big truck" design, used for the popular pickup lines, and adopted it to a large sport utility called Durango. The large and powerful SUVs offer luxurious interiors, big V-8 power, and handsome styling unlike any other American truck.

The second version of the Chrysler, Dodge, Plymouth minivan incorporated improved aerodynamics and a cleaner frontal appearance. Still to be accomplished was the much touted driver-side sliding door.

Tom Gale's design studio was still working with the stretched K-car platforms in the early 1990s and making the very most out of the venerable front-wheel-drive underpinnings. Two of the best efforts were the 1992 Chrysler Fifth Avenue and Imperial, two great nameplates that would fade from the scene when the all-new cab-forward models debuted.

The most exotic of Chrysler concepts and the car almost everyone, including chief stylist Tom Gale, hoped would go into production, the 1995 Atlantic portrayed Chrysler's affection for the classic era. Both the lines of the car and the name were derived from the most famous of all Type 57 Bugattis, the 1935 Atlantic Electron Coupe.

large extent through concept cars. "We always try to fairly predict some things that we may do. Our concept car designs are grounded in reality and people have to step back and wonder whether we're going to do it or not. And if you do a few things that are close, then they can't figure it out at all." You see it in the bold grille design on Ram trucks and Durango, the Jaguaresque nose of the Concorde, in the overall design of the LHS, which varies little in appearance from the 1996 LHX concept vehicle. You see it in the Viper GTS, Prowler, and new PT Cruiser, all of which went into production almost unchanged from the concept cars. Today, Chryslers have *identity*, something long absent from the American automotive scene.

One recent concept car that didn't make the final cut was the Atlantic, which would have made Viper and Prowler seem tame in comparison. The classically inspired styling and even the name were taken from the most revered Bugatti model of the 1930s. "We really wanted to do it. Bob Lutz and I really pushed, but we were at a point in time that we didn't know if we could deliver on the expectations you create with a car like that. Bob was always willing to embrace a new idea, in fact you had to be careful what you showed him because he was so enthusiastic about new ideas. Without him it really would have been tough. He was a great guy to work for."

History will record that Chrysler under the stewardship of Bob Lutz made some remarkable advances in design and technology. Probably in no other environment than the Lutz years at Chrysler could cars like Viper and Prowler have come about.

Recalls Gale of the Viper's development. "Viper was brash, and rude, and it was deliberate that we did it that way because we were learning how to do a limited volume of cars. The Prowler was more refined and took another step, the Viper GTS more refined, and we'd really like to deliver on volume and price with the next one, and make something even more significant than the Atlantic. We have that capability now."

Over the past decade, Chrysler had built an image that consumers respect. The company pioneered the next generation minivan, redefined the sport truck, and brought about a virtual renaissance of the American sports car, sports coupe, and sports sedan, with models like Viper, Prowler, 300M, Concorde, Intrepid, and LHS. Today, there is an entire series of new concept cars, like the Charger R/T (a name reprised from

Dodge's legendary 1970's muscle car), the Plymouth Pronto Spyder, and Chrysler Chronos (a modern interpretation of the great 1953 Chrysler Ghia), that could fill niche markets well into the next decade. "We have to be meaningfully different, we have to offer the customer a viable alternative that is compelling," says Gale. "We've drawn a great deal from our past, bringing back the original Chrysler seal from the 1920s, and using traditional names for many of our concept cars, like Thunderbolt, 300, and Charger. Today, people want some kind of grounding, some heritage, a familiarity, even though things are changing." And this comes shining through in the styling of Chryslers' latest cars.

"We always try to reach for something, so that when you see ours versus the other one, there is a distinction. That was one of the things I had to change when I took over in the mid-1980s," explains Gale. "Chrysler was always on defense in design, we were always being reactive instead of being on offense and being proactive, and one of the first things I did was to tell advance design, 'we're going to be out in front and we're going to just let the rest of the system have to react to us,' and we're doing that to this day." Indeed, there hasn't been a conservative design within the entire Chrysler, Dodge, or Plymouth line-up since 1993, and the wisdom of this has been reflected in sales and profits.

"One of the most gratifying things for us, if you look at this, and use it as a macro measure," says Gale, "was that Chrysler had traditionally been a lagger, in the sense that the average revenue per unit sold was lower than the other domestic competitors. Today the average revenue per unit sold is higher for a Chrysler, and I'm talking across the whole spectrum of our line. Design improved the equity, certainly the market cap, of our company to the point where one of the most prestigious marques in the world would want to be associated and joined with us. That's a real credit to everybody who works at Chrysler. We've still got a long way to go," admits Gale, "but we're proud of what we have been able to do."

Over the past 75 years Chrysler has survived adversity time and again, rebounding from the brink of disaster by reinventing itself at the 11th hour. With the 1998 Daimler-Benz merger, the largest industrial merger in history, the company has assured itself a place in the next century, a place where Tom Gale and the Chrysler design staff can make dream cars come true.

The 1993 Chrysler Concorde introduced America to cab-forward styling and a new generation of Chrysler products developed in Tom Gale's design studio. For Chrysler, the advanced design department was only a few years ahead of production, and what appeared to be pure concept cars in the mid-1990s, like the LHX, were actually sneak previews of real proposals that would be in dealer showrooms by the end of the decade.

Just say "Hi." The Neon took Chrysler into a new arena of sporty subcompact models and into the hearts of a new generation of Chrysler buyers. Penetration of youth market sales dominated by imports like Mazda, Nissan, Toyota, and Honda, was something Chrysler had needed for years. The Neon gave Chrysler that edge.

CHAPTER 11

DAIMLERCHRYSLER
The merger of the century: 2000 and beyond

Today, as it has been since Walter P. Chrysler first lent his name to the company, Chrysler is stretching the limits of conventional design, venturing into niche markets, and redefining the automotive marketplace. From all appearances, the merger with Daimler-Benz on November 12, 1998, has done nothing to alter Chrysler's path. The styling studio still delivers near production-ready concept cars that have an almost unfailing propensity to end up in dealer showrooms. This is Chrysler's classic heritage, the spirit that Walter Percy Chrysler inspired in his company and in his cars three-quarters of a century ago.

There are those who still long for that innocent period when horsepower ruled the road and automakers like Dodge built fire-breathing V-8s stuffed under the hoods of cars with names like Charger R/T. Chrysler would like to do 1970 all over again by paying homage to the muscle car era with the Charger R/T concept car. Under the hood is a 325-horsepower, supercharged 4.7-liter V-8 that runs on compressed natural gas. It's a muscle car that could meet the California Air Resources Board (CARB) Ultra Low Emission Vehicle (ULEV) standard. And don't let those retro body lines fool you. This is a four-door sedan!

Both Chrysler and Daimler-Benz have benefited from their merger in countless ways—an exchange of information, technology, and design that will lead to a remarkable generation of Chrysler, Dodge, Plymouth, and Mercedes-Benz products in the next century.

It begins with the latest models for the year 2000, as the Chrysler marque commences production of its initial twenty-first century models. "The values of distinctive design and innovative engineering that Walter P. Chrysler instilled in the Chrysler brand in 1924 still remain as core principles that define what the Chrysler brand is all about today," says Martin R. Levine, vice president, Chrysler, Plymouth-Jeep Division, Daimler-Chrysler Corporation. "We continue to challenge the convention of the auto industry with products that are at the forefront of their segment with expressive designs, agile handling, athletic performance and practical technology that benefits the customer."

Here then, is a look at the future, the leading Chrysler, Dodge, and Plymouth models for the next century.

CHRYSLER 300M

The 300M rekindles a legacy that began with the first letter car, the Chrysler C-300 in 1955. Now, 45 years later, the letter is M, and the car is magnificent in the tradition of great high-performance Chrysler road cars.

Introduced as an all-new model for 1999, the award-winning 300M enters the 2000 model year with a new 16-inch chrome wheel option for the performance handling package and a new four-disc in-dash compact disc changer with the optional 360-watt Infinity II sound system. New colors for 2000 are dark garnet red, inferno red, shale green metallic, steel blue, and bright silver metallic. Every 300M is equipped with leather-trimmed and heated, eight-way power front seats with a personalized memory system for the driver's seat.

Continuing the legacy of the original letter cars, the Chrysler 300M is powered by a high-output 3.5-liter SOHC V-6 engine rated at 253 horsepower. Chrysler also has a 300-horsepower version on the show car circuit, and if consumer reaction is good, a 2001 model could be in the offing. "No one has asked for a 300M Special," says DaimlerChrysler vice president of design John Hurlitz. "It's just something we wanted to do. We think there's a great place for it in the field. The 300M is an enthusiast car, and it's a logical one to expand upon."

CHRYSLER CONCORDE AND CHRYSLER LHS

Chrysler redefined the full-size sedan segment in 1998 with second generation cab-forward Concorde and LHS models. For year 2000, they continue with the

Chrysler has fixed the only two complaints buyers had about the Concorde: road noise and vibration. The 2000 models feature a new refined touring suspension for a quieter, smoother ride. The highest-performance engine available for the Concorde is an all-aluminum 3.2-liter, 24-valve V-6 developing 225 horsepower.

same leading-edge design and a new refined touring suspension for a quieter, smoother ride, and standard variable-assist, speed-proportional steering on the LXi. The Concorde receives a new gauge design for 2000 with circular instruments and bright gauge bezels.

The highest-performance engine available for the Concorde is Chrysler's all-aluminum 3.2-liter, 24-valve V-6 that generates 225 horsepower. The standard Concorde engine is a 2.7-liter, 24-valve V-6 that delivers 200 horsepower, the best horsepower-per-liter rating in its class. These two aluminum engines are up to 25 percent more powerful and 10 percent more fuel efficient than the previous generation engines used through 1997.

After a complete redesign for 1999, the luxurious Chrysler LHS (which resembles the 1996 Chrysler LHX show car in most every detail) comes standard with virtually every amenity. Chrysler LHS is offered with only three major options: chrome wheels, sunroof, and upgraded Infinity II sound system with four-disc, in-dash CD changer. The host of standard luxury features include heated, leather-trimmed seats, eight-way power front seats, and automatic temperature control air conditioning. The LHS is powered by the same high-performance V-6 used in the 300M, delivering 253 horsepower at 6,400 rpm. Antilock brakes, touring suspension, variable-assist speed sensitive power steering, and low-speed traction control are also standard on the LHS.

CHRYSLER SEBRING COUPE AND CONVERTIBLE

One of the most stylish and successful convertible models in Chrysler history, the 2000 Sebring features new sound insulation to reduce road noise and vibration, and four new exterior colors: shale green metallic, bright silver metallic, black, and taupe metallic. Both the convertible and Sebring coupe are powered by a 2.5-liter SOHC, 24-valve V-6 delivering 168 horsepower at 5,800 rpm.

TOWN & COUNTRY MINIVAN

The Chrysler Town & Country is the ultimate luxury minivan, offered in six long-wheelbase versions for 2000: LX, LXi, LX All-Wheel-Drive (AWD), LXi AWD, and Limited AWD. Top-of-the-line AWD models are powered by Chrysler's 3.8-liter, OHV, 12-valve V-6 coupled to a four-speed automatic transaxle. The 3.8-liter engine delivers 180 horsepower at 4,400 rpm and 240 lb/ft torque at 3,200 rpm.

The sporty Chrysler Sebring convertible is improved for 2000 with new sound insulation to reduce road noise and vibration. There are four new exterior colors, shale green metallic, bright silver metallic, black, and taupe metallic, pictured. Both the Sebring convertible and coupe are powered by a 2.5-liter SOHC, 24-valve V-6 delivering 168 horsepower at 5,800 rpm.

The ultimate luxury minivan is Chrysler's Town & Country Limited. The long wheelbase T&C is available in both two-wheel-drive and full-time all-wheel-drive models for year-round traction control and better foul weather handling.

The Viper GTS-R race car, built for competition in the 1999 American Le Mans series, has spawned a limited production road/race car, the Viper GTS ACR (American Club Racer). Homologated for club racing, the ACR is lighter in weight and stripped for competition (no radio, no air conditioning). All the ACR needs is a roll bar, fire extinguisher, and a driver. (It already comes with racing harnesses and sport seats.) The newest color for the 2000 Viper GTS will be steel gray.

DODGE 2000

Already established as the manufacturer of America's most advanced trucks and sport utility vehicles, Dodge enters the new century with essentially the same products as 1999, though each has refinements to improve handling, comfort, and performance.

The segment-leading Dodge Avenger coupe now features a standard 156-horsepower, 2.5 liter SOHC, 24-valve, V-6 and four-speed automatic transaxle.

For model year 2000, the Dodge Caravan is offered in 11 versions, which include three short-wheelbase models and eight long-wheelbase versions: Caravan, Caravan SE, Caravan Sport, Grand Caravan, Grand Caravan SE, Grand Caravan Sport, Grand Caravan LE, Grand Caravan ES, Grand Caravan Sport All-Wheel Drive (AWD), Grand Caravan LE AWD, and Grand Caravan ES AWD.

The Grand Caravan ES offers AutoStick shifting for either automatic or manually selected gear change in this sportiest of Dodge minivans. The ES also comes with 17-inch aluminum wheels, the largest in this class of

vehicle. Dodge Caravan ES models are powered by a 180-horsepower, 3.8-liter V-6, and AWD models feature four-wheel antilock disc brakes.

Making its debut early in the 2000 calendar year, the powerful Dodge Intrepid R/T features a high-output 3.5-liter SOHC V-6 that delivers 242 horsepower at 6,400 rpm and 250 lb/ft torque at 3,950 rpm, complemented by a selectable dual-mode AutoStick transaxle and tuned performance exhaust. The sporty, cab-forward design Intrepid will also be offered in the standard sedan and ES models that were available in 1999.

The Dodge Neon has been completely redesigned for the year 2000 and features advanced cab-forward styling, jewel headlamps, color-keyed fascias, new rear-end and taillamp design, and more pronounced wheel arches.

"The small car market is extremely competitive as its audience continues to evolve and demand a higher level of refinement," says Tom Gale. "Like its audience, Neon's design has evolved to keep it a segment benchmark, combining fun and features with a solid foundation of best-in-class performance, roominess and handling."

Dodge builds big trucks. One of them is the 2000 Dakota 4x4 quad cab with four real doors, a big cargo bed, and Dodge's trend-setting big truck grille.

New for 2000 is the Durango Sport, a value-priced SUV that comes complete with 40/20/40 split front bench seat, air conditioning, power windows and locks, and five-spoke aluminum wheels. The specially badged Sport is available in chili pepper, patriot blue, flame red (pictured), bright white, black, and bright platinum.

Intrepid, the Dodge counterpart of Chrysler Concorde, will have a special R/T version in 2000 equipped with a high-output 3.5-liter V-6 developing 242 horsepower.

Neon's interior is larger and quieter. The 2000 models feature full-framed doors for a tighter seal to the body, and baked-on mastics and expandable foam baffles were added to reduce noise levels. An exhaust system, featuring a larger muffler and an exhaust flex joint, provides quieter engine operation.

"Neon has been a trendsetter in its market, and that forces us to continue to raise the bar," notes Cindy Hess, DaimlerChrysler vice president, small car platform. "The substance and style of the 2000 Neon is a reflection of where we wanted to take the next generation car. But we made sure that we kept all the fun and sportiness of the original version."

The Dodge Neon R/T will return as a new 2000 model available later in the year. The next Neon R/T will once again claim best-in-class performance, featuring a 150-horsepower, 2.0-liter SOHC engine coupled to a five-speed manual transaxle. With sport suspension—unique springs and sway bars—sporty 16-inch aluminum wheels, and special styling cues—a unique front fascia, front and rear air dams, sill extensions, and a rear spoiler—the 2000 Neon R/T will be the ultimate compact sport sedan. Or will it?

Based on the Neon platform, Chrysler will introduce the 2001 PT Cruiser in early 2000 as a new entry into the specialty vehicle field. Bryan Nesbit, PT Cruiser exterior designer, says, "The Chrysler PT Cruiser borrows design cues from classic American automobiles and interprets them with a healthy dose of American fun and freedom." Notes DaimlerChrysler Chairman Robert J. Eaton, "The PT Cruiser stands

Dodge offers 11 versions of the popular Caravan minivan for model year 2000, including the long-wheelbase Grand Caravan ES. The Grand Caravan ES is also available with all-wheel drive.

alone in the world market because it combines versatility and efficiency wrapped in a distinctly American design." The PT Cruiser is what Eaton calls a "flexible activity vehicle" (a new acronym, FAV) that can lend itself to a variety of uses and styles. Combining the exterior traits of a vintage hot rod and classic panel delivery, the four-door PT measures 168.8 inches in overall length (14 feet), with the interior volume of a full-size sedan.

For North America, the front-wheel-drive PT Cruiser will be powered by a new 2.4-liter DOHC 16-valve engine coupled to either an automatic or manual transmission. Intended as an international model, the PT will be sold overseas in both left- and right-hand drive versions and with a smaller-displacement gas engine or optional diesel.

"The PT Cruiser embodies a design that evokes emotion in people all around the world," says Tom Gale. "The distinct personality of the PT Cruiser is unmatched by any other vehicle on the road." Indeed,

it is a vehicle that will ultimately reflect the personality of the owner in paint schemes, accessories, and as one designer has already envisioned, a woody version. Like Viper and Prowler, the PT will definitely be a vehicle to watch as it matures in the coming decade.

Dodge's ultimate sports car, the Viper GTS ACR will become available to the public in the first quarter of 2000 in a limited production run of 250 to 500 units. "We've learned from the 1998 Viper GT2 commemorative edition that there is a previously untapped demand for limited-production motorsports derivatives of the Viper," says Jim Julow, DaimlerChrysler vice president, Dodge Car and Truck Division. "Racing fuels the desire. Just as the Viper has become the performance icon for the Dodge brand, our Viper GTS-R race car feeds enthusiasm for the street car. In fact, we joined the American Le Mans series in 1999 not only for the excitement it creates among our owners, but also because motorsports plays such an important part in the

The 2000 Dodge and Plymouth Neon are completely new with advanced cab-forward styling, better insulation against noise and vibration, and improved handling. A sports version R/T featuring a 150-horsepower, 2.0-liter SOHC engine coupled to a five-speed manual transaxle will be introduced midseason.

A personal transport is the idea behind the 2001 Chrysler PT Cruiser, due out in the early part of the 2000 model year. Based on the Neon platform, the PT Cruiser is a four-door specialty vehicle that Chrysler Chairman Robert Eaton describes as a "flexible activity vehicle," or FAV. Just what the automotive world needed, a new acronym. Fortunately, the PT Cruiser will make this one worth remembering.

Chrysler has never forgotten the roots of the minivan, the full-size van used for decades by tradesmen. For 2000 there is a full line of Dodge Ram Wagons.

legacy the Viper is building." The Viper GTS ACR (American Club Racer) is a street-legal, yet race-worthy, car group homologated for club racing.

Big trucks keep coming down the road from Dodge, and the latest, the 1998 Durango sport utility, goes into the 2000 model year as one of the best-selling vehicles in its class. "We hit the bull's eye when we developed the Durango," says Bernard Robertson, senior vice president of engineering and technologies and general manager of truck operations. "The availability of a more refined engine as well as improvements to ride and handling will only make Durango a more appealing choice to sport utility vehicle buyers."

Making its debut in Durango four-wheel-drive models for 2000, is the next-generation 4.7-liter Magnum V-8, tuned for even more power, smoothness, and fuel efficiency. It produces 235 horsepower and

295 lb/ft torque. It is coupled to a new fully automatic, electronically controlled transmission with a dual-ratio second gear. For those who require extraordinary levels of power, an optional 5.9-liter Magnum V-8 with 245 horsepower and 335 lb/ft torque will also be available.

The Durango is available in two-wheel drive, or a choice of part time or full time four-wheel-drive models.

Plymouth continues to offer Chrysler's best-priced models for 2000 with the Breeze, 2000 Neon, and Voyager minivans. Prowler continues for another year of limited production and for 2000 a new color, Prowler silver, plus a continuation of Prowler black and Prowler red. Purple and yellow have been retired. Plymouth's production hot rod is powered again by a 253-horsepower, 3.5-liter, SOHC, 24-valve V-6 coupled to an AutoStick four-speed.

WHERE DO WE GO FROM HERE?

There has been more speculation on the future of Chrysler since the merger with Daimler-Benz than there was in the heady days of the great financial bailout. Interestingly, the changes have been subtle, and perhaps will remain so for years to come. Chrysler will have as much to say about future products as Daimler, and the companies have already developed a well-working synergy that was clearly evident at the 1999 Frankfurt motor show. The two top executives, Robert Eaton and Dr. Juergen Schrempp, fielded questions at DaimlerChrysler's first combined motor show on Mercedes' home turf. Chrysler was in the spotlight at Frankfurt and acquitted itself quite well.

While Daimler appears to be the senior partner, which by right of birth it certainly is, the two companies have truly become one, and both have much to

gain from their amalgamation. Increased market share for each in the other's home market being first and foremost, an exchange of engineering and manufacturing technology that will benefit future Chrysler products, and an infusion of the advanced styling that made Chrysler such an attractive partner in the first place, will undoubtedly lead to exciting and new products from both the American and German divisions.

At Frankfurt, Dr. Schrempp noted that by 2001 an investment of $47.7 billion will have been made for new products and developmental projects, which will result in 64 completely new passenger car and commercial vehicles before the 2004 model year. A good percentage of those new vehicles will be Chrysler products.

What does the future hold for Walter P. Chrysler's 75-year-old namesake? The promise of untold possibilities. He would have liked that.

Luxury has no bounds on or off road with the 2000 Grand Cherokee, the sportiest and most lavish SUV in Jeep history.

A HOME FOR THE PAST: A FIRST LOOK AT THE WALTER P. CHRYSLER MUSEUM

BY BARRY DRESSEL

In October 1999, 75 years after the introduction of the first automobile to bear the Chrysler name, DaimlerChrysler opened the Walter P. Chrysler Museum in Auburn Hills, Michigan. Built on the campus of DaimlerChrysler's sprawling North American Headquarters and Chrysler Technical Center (CTC), the 57,000-square-foot museum is a gleaming red granite structure that mirrors the architecture of the CTC complex. Built specially for its purpose, the museum is the first ever opened by an active American automaker. It is intended as a showcase for all the marques associated with the company that Walter P. Chrysler founded, as well as those that preceded it or were part of the American Motors lineage. An exhibition that provides a comprehensive look at Chrysler Corporation and its products—what the company calls "The American Heritage of DaimlerChrysler"—occupies two of the three floors. A third level called "Boss Chrysler's Garage" provides a space for an eclectic gathering of cars, including a "race-track" area devoted to racing and performance vehicles. In all, the museum can show about 70 cars and trucks at a time, from a collection that currently approaches 150 vehicles.

Proud as new parents, company officials are determined to keep the museum fresh by periodically changing exhibits. Another evidence of long-term corporate commitment to the museum is that the collection of vehicles remains the responsibility of the

On the grounds of the magnificent Chrysler Technical Center (CTC) in Auburn Hills, Michigan, the Walter P. Chrysler Museum is the first automotive museum and historical archive ever built specially for the purpose of displaying and preserving an active American automaker's products.

No lack of subtlety. Visitors are wowed from the moment they enter the museum. The two-story high "Tree" holds within its steel branches three significant cars from Chrysler's history, the 1941 Chrysler Thunderbolt, the Chrysler Turbine, and a new Dodge Viper.

engineering department. As a result, virtually every car runs. The museum capitalizes on this fact by periodically pulling cars into a vehicle maintenance area that can be viewed by visitors and firing up the engines, favoring ones like the 1963 Chrysler Turbine, the Viper LeMans car, or the 1917 Willys-Knight V-8, cars that have a distinctive exhaust note.

For those interested in Chrysler history, the museum is a dream come true. Within the company, the idea of a museum was evergreen, but it took the creation of a very visible new headquarters complex in Auburn Hills and the demolition of what display space had existed for the collection at the old Highland Park headquarters to make a museum happen. In some respects, it was a miracle that a vehicle collection still existed to exhibit. Around the time of the loan guarantee in 1980, when every resource that could be sold was being turned into capital, covetous eyes were cast on the collection. At the time, the collection included, among other things, one of six original prototypes of the 1924 Chrysler, a DeSoto Airflow, a first year Plymouth, and assorted other Dodge and Chrysler cars. These cars were "relocated"—that is, hidden—to keep them from being sold. When the company began to prosper again, the collection began to grow—concept cars, antiques bought for use at events, and first editions of vehicles like the K-car, the minivan, and the LeBaron convertible. The acquisition of American Motors in 1987 brought a small group of Hudson, Nash,

History plays an important role in the museum, and in this room Walter P. Chrysler's office has been reconstructed. Walter P. Chrysler is at his desk speaking with his trusted design team, Zeder, Skelton, and Breer.

Rambler, and Jeep vehicles as well, including a 1902 Rambler, a 1909 Hudson, a 1929 Nash with less than 400 miles on it, and assorted other goodies.

When the decision was made to finally build a full-fledged museum and an outline prepared of Chrysler history, it became apparent that however many cars the company had, they did not completely represent the history of Chrysler products. Accordingly, the company assembled a team of engineers—some active, some retired—to locate and restore the cars necessary to tell the Chrysler story. The range of what was needed included everything from classics to muscle cars, concepts to prosaic production successes like the Valiant, the Omni, and the minivan. Jeep products, Dodge trucks, and even a 30-cylinder multibank engine developed by Chrysler to power Sherman tanks were all part of the mix.

By the time the museum was designed and under construction, the acquisition process was in high gear. Generally, the idea was to build a collec-

The main hall exhibit shows a variety of models from Chrysler's 75-year history.

tion of cars with the ideal being to find as many in original condition as possible. When restoration was necessary, as it sometimes inevitably was, the goal was to acquire cars already restored, or source the restoration work. Work by Chrysler's own highly skilled craftsmen was avoided because it generally represented a distraction from regular work on concepts and prototype vehicles. There were exceptions, however. A 1929 DeSoto roadster became a magnificent labor of love. A 1953 Hudson Hornet with the famed "Twin H" six became a ground-up restoration, with a spectacular engine rebuild done by the museum's own mechanics. A call for assistance from the Harry S. Truman Library in Independence, Missouri (Harry S. Truman was a Chrysler fan), resulted in two exquisitely restored 1940 Chryslers, once Truman property. These cars received much attention within the Technical Center, and are now shared between the Truman Library and the Walter P. Chrysler Museum. Other cars received thorough restorations from outside shops under museum supervision, such as the museum's 1955 Chrysler C-300, and the 1948 Town & Country. Among the last cars to be located was a 1953 Chrysler Special, which arrived a few days before top company management reviewed the museum for the first time.

For the former Chrysler Corporation, and for the Chrysler marque, the museum represents the official account. All the Chryslers that should be there are there—the revolutionary 1924 B-60 that started it all, with its powerful six and its classic lines. The big Imperial 8 that led Chrysler into the classic era. The bittersweet Airflow that proved remarkable in every way but public acceptance. The swing-era sophistication of the 1940 Newport and Thunderbolt. The Town & Country, the essence of hunt country chic. Exner/Ghia's hybrid of American engineering with Italian style. The wolf in sheep's clothing that was the first hemi, and the Beautiful Brute that started the famous string of Chrysler 300s. A massive Imperial from 1957 manages to be audacious and dignified at once. The coppery Turbine car still looks to the future, and the Cordoba still speaks of affordable elegance. The modest expectations embodied in the LeBaron convertible are but a few steps from the magnificent retro pizzazz of the Atlantic.

If only Boss Chrysler could see them now.

BIBLIOGRAPHY

Automobile and Culture by Gerald Silk, Henry Flood Robert, Jr., Strother MacMinn, and Angelo Tito Anselmi, 1984, Harry N. Abrams, Inc., N.Y. Publisher

Automobile Quarterly Vol. 32, No. 4., Kutztown, Pennsylvania

Chrysler Chronicle by James M. Flammang, 1998, Publications International, Ltd., Lincolnwood, Illinois

Collector Cars by Lee Culpepper, 1989, Octopus Books Ltd., London

80 Years of Cadillac LaSalle by Walter M. P. McCall, 1982, Crestline Publishing

100 Years of the World's Automobiles, 1962, G. N. Georgano, Floyd Clymer Publications

Pace Cars of the Indy 500 by L. Spencer Riggs, Speed Age Inc.

70 Years of Chrysler by George H. Dammann, 1974, Crestline Pub., MBI Publishing Company, Osceola, Wisconsin

Speed & Luxury—The Great Cars by Dennis Adler, 1997, MBI Publishing Company, Osceola, Wisconsin

Standard Catalog of American Cars, 1805–1942 by Beverly Rae Kimes and Henry Austin Clark, Jr., 1985, Krause Publications, Iola, Wisconsin

The Illustrated Encyclopedia of the World's Automobiles by David Burgess Wise, 1979, Quarto Publishing, Chartwell Books, Inc.

The World Guide to Automobile Manufacturers by Nick Baldwin, G. N Georgano, Michael Sedgwick, and Brian Laban, 1987, Macdonald & Co., London

APPENDIX

DaimlerChrysler Timeline
Compiled by Barry Dressel, manager, Walter P. Chrysler Museum

HISTORIC TIMELINE

1900–1909

The Edwardian Era—the transition from Victoria's nineteenth century to the twentieth. In 1901, the year the Dodges go into the machine shop business, Queen Victoria (b. 1819) dies and William McKinley—last U.S. president to serve in the Civil War—is assassinated. Americans are a rural people who travel by horse, train, and electric trolley. They get used to mechanized individual transport on the bicycle. Two bicycle mechanics build the first successful powered heavier-than-air flying machine. A fellow inhabitant of Dayton, Ohio, develops an electric self-starter for cars, eliminating cranking, and making driving more feasible for women. Pianos rival bathtubs in popularity, people go to see vaudeville. Baseball is barely a professional sport, basketball is just invented, football merely a college game. After defeating Spain in 1898, the United States is perceived as a world power. Thousands of new cars are introduced, but Henry Ford will introduce the Model T in 1908 (at an unheard-of low price of $850 equipped). The American approach to the automobile—cheap, utilitarian, mass-produced—is firmly established, but cars still look like horse-drawn open coaches. The bodies are varnished, and take weeks to finish. Oil reserves found at Spindletop, near Beaumont, Texas, ensure plenty of cheap gasoline. Men smoke cigars or chew, only boys "sip" at cigarettes. Lung cancer is a rare disease. Men and women wear high-topped shoes, women's dresses are ankle length, men wear three-piece suits and carry pocket watches. The preferred look is fleshy—President Taft weighs over 300 pounds, and Lillian Russell over 200 pounds. Everyone wears hats, men using straw "skimmers" in summer.

1910–1919

Woodrow Wilson is the last president to ride to his inaugural in a carriage (1912) the year after the biggest ocean liner yet built (*Titanic*) sinks on its maiden voyage, an event heralded as the end of the Victorian era. The United States ends more than a century of isolation to enter a European war. It is a war in which men are killed by gas and machine guns, ocean liners carrying civilians are torpedoed without warning by submarines, and airplanes engage in dogfights. London is bombed from the air. Michigan is the major producer of automobiles, and Henry Ford, building millions of Model Ts at ever-lower prices, is intent on improving the lot of the farmer. His decree of $5 a day minimum wages creates a riot among job seekers. Babe Ruth is a baseball pitcher, movies are competing with vaudeville, people are listening to disk records on Victrolas, dancing to ragtime, and Europe is in debt to the United States. The American approach to the automobile is becoming standardized—gas-fueled internal combustion engine, four-cylinder minimum, self-starter, geared transmission, rear drive. Cars still look like they need horses. Polio and influenza appear after the war.

1920–1929

America is for the first time predominantly urban, not rural. Americans try Prohibition. Women bob their hair, hike their skirts, and show their legs through silk stockings. They move toward a boyish figure. They can vote. They smoke cigarettes. Men still favor cigars—Sinclair Lewis' George F. Babbit is very proud of the cigar lighter accessory on his car. Men and women wear bathing suits that show their whole bare legs. Women start to wear Dacron slips. Men wear fedoras and celluloid collars. Nitrocellulose paint is introduced in 1923, and the time to paint cars drops dramatically. Henry drops the price on the open Model T two-seater under $300—less than half what the car cost when introduced 15 years before. Closed cars are ever more popular (vide Essex 1922) and are the majority of new registrations by the time Charles Lindbergh flies nonstop and solo, New York to Paris (1927). That same year (1) the Model T, hopelessly obsolete, dies, having put American on wheels, and (2) GM hires Harley Earl to "style" the LaSalle. Looks matter, and Henry Ford makes sure to "make a lady out of Lizzie" when he introduces the Model A. The same year (1928), Chrysler introduces the Plymouth. Americans discover not only sex, but the fact that cars—especially closed cars—can be mobile bedrooms. Ned Jordan sells his car with sex. Alfred Sloan rationalizes General Motors, decreeing a car for every pocketbook—Herbert Hoover will promise "two chickens in every pot, and a car in every garage." Americans demand cars with six cylinders and good roads to drive them on. Walter Chrysler and deposed GM founder W. C. Durant launch the last two multimarque auto corporations. Durant's will die in the Depression. Railroad and trolley track mileage peaks. Movies are killing vaudeville, radio is a sensation, Babe Ruth is a home run king, Rudy Valle and Gene Austin sell millions of records. Ragtime gives way to jazz and people do the Charleston and the lindy hop. Franklin Roosevelt, a former Democratic vice presidential nominee, develops polio. Insulin is isolated. Leaded gas—what a good idea. In Germany, two respected auto companies merge, and two German auto pioneers die.

1930–1939

The Depression is real. Prohibition is repealed. Babe Ruth will retire. Football is organized. Franklin Roosevelt, a polio victim, will fly from New York to Chicago to accept the Democratic nomination in 1932. In 1936 the March of Dimes will be founded. Men have adopted wristwatches, double-breasted suits, low shoes, and cigarettes. Following Clark Gable's example, undershirts become old fashioned. They stop wearing bathing suits with tops, too. They smoke cigarettes now—FDR's jaunty cigarette holder is famous. All the midrange car companies introduce eight-cylinder cars. Luxury makes struggle, and Pierce, Stutz, Franklin, Auburn—die. Cadillac boosts sales by crossing a color line and having GMAC offer credit to black Cadillac buyers. Ford introduces a low-priced V-8, but by 1936 will be third behind GM and Chrysler. In 1936 the merged German auto company introduces a diesel-powered car. Radio and film are the dominant entertainment. People jitterbug to big bands that play swing. The UAW will be created and will successfully organize GM and Chrysler in reaction to wage cuts, speed-ups, and brutal work conditions—Ford will follow in 1941. DuPont introduces Nylon, which speedily replaces silk in women's hosiery, and women wearing it ponder Clarence Birdseye's new frozen foods. Railroads experiment with diesels, and Douglas introduces the first modern airliner, the DC-3. GM offers diesel buses to replace trolleys. Everything is streamlined, Chrysler introduces the Airflow, and Hupmobile the same year offers a streamlined Loewy design. Cars look like cars, and the last vestiges of wood in car bodies vanish. In the 1936 Cord, Gordon Buehrig designs an icon.

1940–1949

After entering yet another world war late, America emerges the dominant world power, and, until decade's end, the only nuclear power. A small two-piece women's bathing suit is named after the site of a nuclear bomb test. FDR dies in office, and Harry S. Truman is a Chrysler fan. People are worried about Communism. Penicillin and other antibiotics developed during the war permit control of TB and STDs, but lung cancer is rising due to cigarette smoking. Pennsylvania started the decade by opening the first modern turnpike. Train travel and trolley use are down, and the suburbs typified by Levittown are a cliché. Detroit dusts off its prewar designs, and they look old. Studebaker

beats everyone to the market with a new design, and most of the designs that follow are streamlined bathtubs. Chrysler, fingers still sore from the Airflow, is the most conservative, but makes points with its T&C convertibles. Oldsmobile starts a horsepower race with a new overhead-valve V-8, and Cadillac offers fins inspired by the P-38. Teenagers are bobbysoxers, and they dance to bop. Basketball gets organized, stock car racing is growing, and the Yankees dominate baseball. People are beginning to buy televisions.

1950–1959

The Fabulous Fifties. It starts by worrying about Communists in Korea, and ends worrying about Communists in Cuba. Americans are making ever more money, which they spend to buy bigger, gaudier, and faster cars, with more gadgets. A GM designer says his favorite color is chrome. Photographs of car designers feature them looking sophisticated, and, like Edward R. Murrow, they hold cigarettes. Lung cancer is a national concern. John Wayne and Arthur Godfrey lose lungs. But Salk invents a polio vaccine. Chrysler misses the boat on styling at first, and falls behind Ford and GM, but produces the ace in the horsepower race with the introduction of the hemi in 1951. Chrysler lures Virgil Exner from the Loewy tribe at Studebaker, and by 1955 has produced cars that look like—and are said to have looks like—a hundred-million dollars. He calls it the Forward Look. Chrysler drops a 300-horsepower hemi in one to create a sophisticated performance car. The hundred-million-dollar look gives way to finned cars, Chrysler's entries in the age of excess. The iconic design of the era is, however, the 1953 Studebaker Commander Starlite Coupe. The horsepower and gadget race and the plethora of models is tough on the independents, and tough on the midrange cars, a market GM has sewn up. Packard goes, Kaiser/Willys settles for Jeeps, Studebaker and DeSoto are dying, Edsel flops, Hudson is absorbed, and Nash becomes a Rambler again that George Romney dubs a compact. More compact still is the VW Beetle which famously and heretically suggests that drivers think small and avoid lemons. Irritated by this German poacher on native turf, the Big Three plot their response. It is a good time to be an assembly line worker. Profits are high, and after some bitter strikes early in the decade, fatter labor contracts become more and more ritualized. Meanwhile, neighborhood movie houses suffer as America discovers it loves Lucy at home on the TV. They eat TV dinners as they watch. America launches the ultimate ocean liner in the same decade that trans-Atlantic passenger jet travel is inaugurated. We build a nuclear navy. Train and trolley companies are suffering. President Eisenhower creates the Interstate Highway System. Cities are losing population. A former Tennessee truck driver scandalizes the nation on CBS' *Ed Sullivan Show*, and teenagers look like delinquents as they embrace rock 'n roll. Cotillions now teach three basic jitterbug steps. Patti Page's career has peaked. Records are 45-rpm plastic. People play them on record players that are Hi Fi—high fidelity sound. A milkshake mixer salesman named Ray Kroc buys out a pair of hamburger stand operators named McDonald, whose wares are sold under Golden Arches. People crane their necks from inside their convertibles to see if they can see Sputnik and Vanguard. Civil rights becomes a color-coded issue. Hugh Hefner makes a sex magazine a lifestyle. Anything with transistors must be good.

1960–1969

The United States inaugurates its first president born in the twentieth century and fails to expel Communism from either Cuba or Southeast Asia. A president smokes cigars, and publicly eschews hats. American men follow suit. No one wears double-breasted suits anymore. A women's fashion designer eschews covered breasts and the term "topless" is attached to "bathing suit." Civil rights activists become more militant. A president and his brother, and two civil rights leaders are assassinated. Another president "skinny dips" in the White House. We import ever more petroleum from abroad. We begin to import rock music from England. We import more small cars—but no one wants a car from Japan. A VW Beetle is less than $1,900. Another sort of Beatle comes from England and sings. People look up psychedelic in the dictionary, and nice kids experiment with drugs. Rock musicians make their guitars louder, distort the sounds, and destroy them on stage. People sing protest songs. Motown means music of a different sort. Records are increasingly 33.3 rpm long-playing disks—LPs. They play them on what they call "stereos." People watch *The Beverly Hillbillies* on television. GM drops a big engine in a small Pontiac, and calls it GTO. Performance means muscle. Gas is cheap. Seatbelts are standard. Chrysler sees the last of Exner and slices off his fins as soon as he leaves. GM designer Bill Mitchell—father of the Buick Riviera and the Corvette Stingray—complains that designing a compact car is like tailoring for a dwarf. The pony car debuts, and the market gets ever more segmented. Trolley systems are dying, and passenger train service is very sick. There are two and more car families. There is concern about smog, pollution, and health. The Big Three are obsessed with power and production, not road manners or fit and finish. The enduring designs are the Stingray and another Loewy design (the Avanti) is Studebaker's supernova. It goes on without Studebaker. We can do guns and butter. Richard Nixon promises to bring us together. Civil rights gets a radical chic edge. Workers learn that cybernation means automation. UAW's Walter Reuther looks at a robot and comments that it doesn't buy cars. Man walks on the moon. Cigarettes get a surgeon general's warning. Birth control pills transform lifestyles. Hearts are transplanted.

1970–1979

Walter Reuther dies. We declare the war in Asia won and go home. Vietnam collapses. An expletive deleted, Richard Nixon resigns. Rock bands play stadiums. Janis Joplin, Jimi Hendrix, Jim Morrison, Marvin Gaye, and Elvis Presley give us days the music dies. Bruce Springsteen is proclaimed the music's

new day. Women demand equal rights and an amendment to ensure it. Suits seem stuffy, and ties grow flowers. Bras are burned. A man named Comfort writes about the Joy of Sex. This is news? The Beetle goes, but the Japanese are eating the vineyard. Gas is suddenly not cheap anymore. Pollution is a serious issue, and "catalytic converters" enter the motorist's vocabulary, along with "55 mile per hour limit." Leaded gas leaves us. William Mitchell's dwarf, the Corvair, is indicted for being unsafe at any speed. GM and Chrysler bring out front-wheel-drive economy cars. A small Chrysler with Corinthian leather is hailed, but Chrysler staggers towards bankruptcy. The car has a stereo radio that also plays a type of cassette tape called eight-track. At home people buy "stereo component systems" to play music. They watch *All in the Family* on televisions that are hooked up to cable systems. Honda offers the Accord, and Toyota the Corona—dwarfs no longer. The Volvo station wagon is a status symbol. People look at price stickers and get "sticker shock." If it's turbo, it must be good, and painted matte black. Jimmy Carter wears a sweater during a fireside chat. Inflation is rampant. Americans are hostages in Iran. No one really thinks Americans could use computers at home.

1980–1989

America elects its last president born before World War I, and its last born before World War II. John Lennon is murdered. Communism dies. Chrysler nearly dies, and crawls back with a federal loan guarantee so it can borrow money. The K-cars debut, to be endlessly reheated. One rehash: Convertibles, virtually extinct, come back, with great success. One rehash becomes a banquet, the minivan. Quality matters, and amidst premortem obituaries, the American auto companies get religion. They also, for the first time in several decades, discover the joys of four- and six-cylinders. Front-wheel drive goes from oddity to virtually compulsory. Small cars are good. Chrysler replaces ancient plants, and Lee Iacocca suggests you buy a better car if you can find it. He smokes a cigar, but you can't smoke on an airplane anymore. GM decides to build a new car in a new way, but begins to lose a once-commanding level of dominance in the domestic industry. Ford introduces a new car in a style that is derided by some of the old stylists elsewhere as "the flying potato." The flying potato has the competition for lunch, and suddenly sharp edges are gone, chrome is no one's favorite color, and wire hubcaps and landau irons are corny. Ronald Reagan announces that it is morning in America, again. People embrace casual Fridays at work. Children are asked to just say no. Americans learn what AIDS stands for and also worry about second-hand smoke. People discover and forget disco. They rediscover ballroom dancing and are fascinated by the lambatta and the tango. They listen to private "Walkman" style FM radios. They buy cassette tapes of music instead of recorded disks. Some buy a new disk called a compact disk, a CD. Some begin playing these disks on home computers. People watch *MASH* on television. Everyone buys video cassette players, and the movie industry becomes

1990s

We elect our first president born after World War II. We learn what SUV stands for. Big is back. Power is fun. Lee Iacocca retires and is succeeded by Robert Eaton. The president smokes cigars. So does Jerry Seinfeld. Chrysler's vice chairman is a vegetarian who smokes cigars. Women rate Chrysler as a great place to work. Japan, Inc., is sick, and so is Chrysler, ailing with stale products. Chrysler proceeds to dazzle everyone with an unprecedented string of design and market successes. Exciting concept cars—one with a humidor for cigars—suddenly yield equally exciting products. Luxury sport utilities from Jeep and Dodge. Specialty image cars like Viper from Dodge and Prowler from Plymouth. Aggressively styled pickups from Dodge. A V-10 engine. The LH cars debut, laying to rest the taunt that LH stands for "Last Hope." Instead everyone learns what "cab forward" means. A bigger version, the LHS, also wins applause. A new minivan edition is hailed as the design standard and is named "Car of the Year" even though it's a minivan. A new small car appears and wins acclaim and success in what was considered an impossible market segment for an American maker. Midsized cars win design awards. Quality soars. The LH and LHS models are restyled, and Chrysler is the acknowledged design leader. The 300 series is resurrected; the new edition is a "5 meter car" designed to be marketable in Europe; it is a domestic success and another "Car of the Year." The head of Chrysler design likes double-breasted suits. All the cars have compact disk players and multiple speakers. Cigarette lighters are now "power points." Chrysler is considered the most nimble, creative, and profitable American car company. The chairman sees "A Perfect Storm" facing the global automotive industry. To assure its future in this ever-more-competitive industry, Chrysler merges with Daimler-Benz, the world leader in automotive technology and quality, to form DaimlerChrysler. Cigars all 'round, but you can't smoke them in California restaurants. You can dance to swing music, though.

DaimlerChrysler Lineage

MAXWELL-CHALMERS

1897—Bicycle manufacturer Albert Augustus Pope (1843–1909), maker of Columbia bicycles, begins manufacturing gas and electric vehicles under brand name Columbia.

1899—Pope's Columbia brand merges into Electric Vehicle Company.

1903—Maxwell-Briscoe founded by Benjamin Briscoe (1869–1945) and Jonathan Maxwell (1864–1928).

—E. R. Thomas (1850–1936) founds Thomas in Buffalo, New York.

1904—Stoddard Dayton founded. Thomas is now Thomas Flyer. Alden Sampson founded to make cars. Alden Sampson switches to trucks. Thomas Detroit offshoot is begun by Roy D. Chapin (1880–1936) and Howard Coffin, both later to found Hudson. Frank Briscoe, brother of Benjamin (1875–1954), and Alanson P. Brush found Brush to build the wood-framed Brush Runabout.

1908—A Thomas Flyer wins the New York to Paris race. Thomas Detroit discontinued in favor of Chalmers Detroit.

—Hugh Chalmers (1873–1932) dies.

1909—Electric Vehicle Company, which has always made gas and electric cars, has name change, to Columbia. Alden Sampson sold to United Motors.

1910—Benjamin Briscoe forms United Motors out of Columbia, Brush, Maxwell-Briscoe, and 130 smaller firms.

—Chalmers Detroit becomes Chalmers.

1912—United Motors collapses.

1912–1913—Columbia markets Columbia-Knight with sleeve-valve engine.

1913—Hugh Chalmers founds Saxon.

1914—Jonathan Maxwell reorganizes Maxwell Briscoe into Maxwell Motors—only firm to emerge from United Motors.

1915—Saxon bought from Chalmers (Saxon expires, 1922).

1921—The Good Maxwell.

1922—Chalmers merges with Maxwell.

—Chalmers discontinued.

1925—Last Maxwell.

WILLYS

1903—Overland founded.

1909—Company renamed Willys-Overland (John North Willys, 1873–1933). W-O acquires Pope Toledo.

—Paige-Detroit is organized.

1911—Paige-Detroit becomes simply Paige.

1913—Duesenberg brothers (Fred and August) organize Duesenberg Motors to build auto and marine engines, not cars.

1914—Willys Knight founded. Company is second largest producer after Ford.

1919—Willys buys out the Duesenbergs for the sake of their Elizabeth, New Jersey, factory—when engineers Zeder, Skelton, Breer, and Walter Chrysler plan a new Chrysler six-cylinder car to be introduced by Willys. This is the plant in which they intend to produce it. Because of Willys' financial problems, this plant will be auctioned in 1922 along with the Chrysler prototype—the plant had a sign on it saying it was the home of Chrysler, the Six-Cylinder Car—and bought by William C. Durant to be part of Durant Motors. The car debuts as the Flint in 1923 and lasts until 1927.

1925—Stearns Knight purchased.

1927—Whippet and Falcon Knight (companion cars) produced.

1928—Paige becomes Graham-Paige (see Graham brothers under Dodge).

1929—Stearns Knight and Falcon Knight discontinued.

1930—Willys six introduced. Graham-Paige becomes Graham.

1931—Whippet discontinued in favor of Willys name.

1933—Willys Model 77 (small car with floating power) introduced—cheapest car in United States except for Austin Bantam, and successful as a racing car. —Willys-Knight discontinued.

1935—John North Willys dies.

1938—U.S. Army RFP for light recon vehicle to replace motorcycle and sidecars commonly used.

1939—Willys develops concept drawings.
—Overland name is revived.

1940—Willys delivers two prototypes, both with two- or four-wheel drive, one with four-wheel steering.
—Overland renamed Americar.

1941—Willys unit accepted, incorporating modifications from submissions by Ford and American Bantam. First units produced of eventual 368,000 from Willys and 232,000 from Ford.

1945—First civilian model Jeep CJ2A.

1945—Kaiser Motors set up to produce Kaiser and Frazer automobiles.

1946—Jeep station wagon appears. First Kaisers and Frazers sold (1947 models).

1947—All assets of Graham Motors (controlled since 1944 by Joseph Frazer) are transferred to Kaiser Frazer.

1948—First Jeepster produced.

1950—Henry J compact introduced by Kaiser. Jeepster discontinued.
—Jeep trademark is registered in United States and internationally.

1951—Frazer discontinued, Kaiser restyled.

1952—Willys car reintroduced (in addition to Jeeps).

1954—Kaiser acquires Willys, thereafter known as Kaiser-Willys Motors. Henry J discontinued. Kaiser Darrin sports car introduced (one year). CJ5 Jeep introduced—remains in production until 1983.

1955—Kaiser and Willys marques discontinued—hereafter only Jeeps, as a product of Willys Motors of Kaiser Industries Corp.

1962—Jeep Wagoneer introduced.

1963—Willys Motors becomes Kaiser Jeep. V-6 appears on CJs.

1970—Quadrotrac introduced.
—American Motors acquires Jeep, makes it Jeep Corporation, a subsidiary of AMC.

1972—AMC-built V-8s available on Jeep vehicles.

1974—Jeep Cherokee debuts.

1984—Cherokee XJ introduced, named "4x4 of Year" by three off-road magazines.

1986—Jeep Wrangler introduced.

1987—AMC and AMC Jeep bought by Chrysler Corporation. Second-largest American automobile industry merger in history.

1992—Grand Cherokee introduced.

HUDSON

1909—First Hudson, Model 20, introduced.

1912—Joseph L. Hudson dies. Hudson Super Six introduced. First Essex (a 1919 model) introduced as companion car to Hudson—an inexpensive, high-performance (for the time) 55-horsepower four-cylinder engine.

1922—Essex a closed car for only $300 more than a touring car.

1925—The coach was $5 less than a touring car.

1930—First Hudson 8.

1932—Essex becomes Essex Terraplane.

1933—Essex name dropped, Terraplane gets the Hudson 8—the high power-to-weight ratio produces sensational performance and speed records.

1936—Hudson President Roy D. Chapin dies.

1937—Terraplane phased out.
—Step-down design used on Hudson for the first time.

1953—Hudson Jet compact introduced. This model's disappointing sales convince Hudson that merger is necessary. Some Hudsons equipped for "severe usage" develop 200 horsepower and dominate stock car racing.

NASH

1902—Thomas Jeffery sells the first Rambler.

1914—Jeffery introduces the Quad, a four-wheel-drive, four-wheel-steering truck with steering at each end. Rambler cars are renamed Jeffery, in founder's honor.

1917—Charles Nash buys Jeffery. Nash is car's new name, new models feature OHV engines; Nash is world's leading producer of trucks.

1921—Nash launches high-priced Lafayette.

1924—Lafayette discontinued; the wrong car at the wrong time.

1925—Lower-priced Ajax marque produced.

1926—Ajax made into the Nash Light Six.

1929—Nashes are given twin ignition when ordered with OHV engine—this unique feature lasts to 1940.

1932—Only GM and Nash make money; Nash out-earns GM.

1934—LaFayette name revived for low-cost line.

1937—Nash buys Kelvinator to secure services of its president, George W. Mason.

1941—Nash 600 replaces LaFayette; has unitized body and low price, major success.

1948—Charles Nash dies. Succeeded by George Mason.

1949—Nash Airflyte introduced.

1950—Compact Rambler introduced.

1952—"Golden Airflytes" styled by famed Italian designer Sergio "Pinin" Farina. Nash Healey sports car debuts, built by Nash, engineered by Donald Healey, and designed by Pinin Farina.

1952—Nash Metropolitan introduced.

1954—Merger of Hudson and Nash creates American Motors.
  —President George Mason dies, succeeded by George Romney.

1956—Nash Cross Country Wagon is first "hardtop" (no B pillar).
  —Rambler compact dropped, name applied to new larger car.

1958—Nash name dropped from full-sized line (although Romney considers these compacts) in favor of Rambler, the old subcompact known as Rambler reappears after a hiatus as the Rambler American.

1962—George Romney resigns as AMC president to campaign for and win Michigan governorship.

1963—Entire AMC line named "Car of the Year" by *Motor Trend*.

1968—Javelin and AMX introduced.

1970—Hornet replaces Rambler American. The Hornet subsequently is calved (and then chopped) to make the Gremlin, the Eagle, and the Concorde. Gremlin is first U.S.-built subcompact.

1975—Pacer, first U.S. wide subcompact.

1980—Eagle four-wheel-drive passenger car is introduced. Renault buys minority share in AMC.

1983—Renault Alliance introduced.

DODGE

1901—John (1864–1920) and Horace (1868–1920) found a machine shop after selling out of Evans and Dodge Bicycle business. Soon they are supplying engines to Olds; in 1903 they become 10 percent owners of new Ford Motor Company in return for supplying engines and transmissions. In 1913, afraid that Ford will become self-sufficient, they give Ford a year's notice of withdrawal from their contract, and announce a car of their own. In 1919 Ford will eventually buy the Dodge Brother's original $20,000 worth of stock for $25 million, making them two of the wealthiest men in America.

1914—First Dodge car, Model 30-35, four-cylinder.

1915—Dodge cars are used in combat—the U.S. Army's first gasoline-powered combat vehicles—against Pancho Villa in Mexico.

1916—Graham Brothers start putting truck bodies on Dodge car chassis.

1917—Dodge commercial vehicles appear as 1918 models.

1920—Both John and Horace Dodge die. Frederick Haynes becomes president in 1921.

1921—Dodge allows the Graham Brothers (Ray 1887–1932, Robert 1885–1967, Joseph 1883–1971), truck body builders, to build trucks under the Graham name with Dodge running gear and engines exclusively; six months later Dodge buys controlling interest in Graham; the Brothers leave in 1927 to turn Paige into Graham-Paige and build cars.

1923—Dodge introduces first all-steel four-door sedans. Dodge Brother's heirs sell company to the banking firm of Dillon, Read and Co. for $146 million. Dodge assumes control of Graham.

1927—Dodge's first six-cylinder model is introduced.

1928—Dodge is bought by Chrysler Corporation (same year Chrysler began building trucks in Canada under the Fargo name, which will become the Dodge truck name in Canada after acquisition by Chrysler). Dodge purchase is largest automotive merger in U.S. history up to that time. Internal expanding hydraulic brakes are introduced on Dodge. Integral floorpan bodies—forerunner of unitized bodies.

1930—Dodge introduces straight-eight engine. No more Graham Brothers trucks.

1933—First Chrysler-engineered Dodge trucks. Dodge Ram symbol appears.

1935—Dodge custom builds Airflow styled tank trucks (until 1940).

1936—Dodge revives the convertible sedan.

1938—Last year for Dodge Brothers insignia.

1939—"Job-rated" redesigned Dodge trucks appear; special Hayes-bodied coupes appear.

1945—Dodge introduces the "Power Wagon" truck—the civilian version of a military truck.

1948—"Pilot house" Dodge pickups appear.

1953—First Dodge V-8.

1956—Dodge "Sweptside" truck introduced.
  —Dodge Daytona 500 hemi model introduced.

1961—First all-new Dodge truck.

1963—Subcompact Dart.

1964—Dodge A400 van.

1969—Dodge Charger Daytona.

1973—Dodge Club Cab pickup.

1978–1979—Dodge introduces the Li'l Red Express (7,200 total built).

1992—Dodge Viper.

1994—Dodge Ram truck.

CHRYSLER/PLYMOUTH/DESOTO

1922—A reworked Maxwell appears with improved engine and chassis. Maxwell and Chalmers merge.

1923—Walter P. Chrysler, managing Willys-Overland, takes on Maxwell and Chalmers. Maxwell rear axle reengineered and sold as "Good Maxwell." Chalmers discontinued.

1924—First Chrysler model produced by Maxwell-Chalmers Motors.

1925—Maxwell-Chalmers is reorganized as Chrysler Corporation. Last Maxwells built. Chrysler Canada organized. Balloon tires standard.

1926—Maxwell is now Chrysler 58, a four-cylinder model. The Imperial is introduced, bigger than the Chrysler, with larger engine and distinctive styling. Chrysler Limited (UK) organized. Chrysler 50 appears, the basis for Plymouth.

1928—Privately sponsored Chrysler places third overall at LeMans.
—Dodge Brothers acquired.
—Plymouth replaces Chrysler 50, and DeSoto introduced as new model. Downdraft carburetion, internal expanding hydraulic brakes, Lovejoy shocks as standard equipment.

1930—DeSoto and Dodge eights introduced. Chrysler eights introduced. Floating power appears on 1932 model Plymouths. Ads feature Walter P. and the slogan "Look At All Three!" as Plymouth reaches number three production spot. All models have floating power. Plymouth offers IFS and six cylinders. All cars have helical gear transmissions.

1934—Chrysler and DeSoto Airflows. Airstream Chryslers introduced due to poor Airflow sales.

1936—Half-million Plymouths manufactured this year. K. T. Keller is president of Chrysler.

1938—Walter Chrysler is ill, retires from company chairmanship.
—Fabricas Automex (Mexico) established. Chrysler offers "New York Special" for one year. Robert Cadwallader is new head stylist.

1939—Last Dietrich-styled cars. Chrysler introduces Windsor, New Yorker, and Saratoga series. Bearings are superfinished. Safety Signal speedometers and column shifts introduced.

1940—Walter Chrysler dies.
—Thunderbolt and Newport show cars are shown. Newport chosen as 1941 Indy 500 Pace Car. Safety rim wheels introduced.

1941—Last models (year 1942) are produced without plated trim, due to strategic need for chrome.

1942—DeSotos have hidden headlamps. Production stops for war. By war's end, Chrysler will have produced, among other things, 397,209 trucks, 25,507 tanks, three billion cartridges, and 175,000 engines of all types.

1945—Reconversion to car production begins in July, Chrysler begins production in December.

1946—Town and Country convertible and sedan introduced, replacing wagon.

1949—As a "Second Series," the corporation offers restyled cars.
—Virgil Exner joins Chrysler.

1950—Keller becomes chairman—first since WPC's death—and "Tex" Colbert is president.

1951—Hemi engine introduced, and power steering.

1952—Hemis compete (in Cunninghams) at LeMans and on the stock car circuit. DeSotos also equipped with hemi engines.

1953—Dodge gets a hemi, a Cunningham is third at LeMans; d'Elegance show car is shown. First Chrysler fully automatic transmission.

1954—Dodge, DeSoto, and Plymouth get automatic transmissions.

1955—First year of the "Forward Look," first Chrysler 300, first Plymouth V-8, Imperial a separate make.

1957—"Flite Sweep" styling offers fins, low profile created by use of torsion bar instead of spring suspension. Highest market share for next 39 years.

1958—Chrysler purchases share in SIMCA. SIMCA began in 1934 by building the Fiat Balilla in France. The SIMCA 5 (Fiat Topolino) and the SIMCA 8 (Fiat 508C Balilla) followed, both Airflow influenced. In 1950 came the SIMCA 9, which became the SIMCA Aronde and lasted until the mid-1960s. In the mid-1950s SIMCA acquired Ford France. SIMCA Horizon is the inspiration for the American version.

1959—Wedges replace the hemis. SIMCAs are imported for U.S. sale.

1960—Valiant debuts. Everything but Imperial is unibody built. Slant six replaces flathead six. Valiants feature alternator. William Newburg succeeds Colbert, who moves to chairman. Newburg lasts two months. Townsend succeeds Newburg. Valiant dominates short-lived compact stock car class.

1961—Dodge version of Valiant is the Lancer; DeSoto discontinued.
—Colbert resigns as chairman, succeeded by George Love, Virgil Exner replaced by Elwood Engel.

1963—Chrysler builds 50 turbine-powered cars.

1963—Dart compact debuts. Five-year/50,000-mile warranty introduced.

1964—The Barracuda beats the Mustang to market by two weeks, Richard Petty takes a first at Daytona in a hemi Plymouth. Chrysler buys a share in Rootes Group and controlling interest in SIMCA. Hillman was founded 1871 to build bicycles (first car 1907) and controlled after 1928 by the Rootes Brothers. Humber, formed by Thomas Humber about 1900, bought Commer Cars Ltd., who were, rather confusingly, truck builders. In 1928, Humber bought Hillman as Rootes was formed. Humber known for the late-1930s Humber Snipe and Super Snipe models, which lasted until 1964.
—Sunbeam, like Hillman and Humber, was originally a bicycle maker who produced its first car in 1900. In 1923 a Sunbeam became the first British car to win a Grand Prix. Associated with Talbot-Darracq from

France, Sunbeam became part of Rootes after Sunbeam-Talbot-Darracq collapsed in 1935. The French remainder became Talbot-Lago, later part of SIMCA. Americans best-know Sunbeam for the Sunbeam Alpine.

—Singer, another bicycle maker, built its motorized tricycle in 1901 and its first car in 1905. Singer predated the Airflow with a concept called Airstream, and in 1948 built a model called the SM1500, which became the Singer Hunter in 1955 and featured a SOHC engine. They joined Rootes in 1956. The Singer Hunter eventually became the Hillman Hunter.

1965—Dodge Hemi-Charger and Plymouth SuperStock debut.

1966—"Street hemi" offered.

1967—Lynn Townsend chairman of the board, Virgil Boyd president. Dodge Coronet R/T and Plymouth Belvedere GTX introduced. Richard Petty wins NASCAR championship in a Plymouth. Dodge Super Bee introduced. First year for federal emission controls.

1969—First year of fuselage styling. Dodge Charger Daytona built for stock car racing. A 440 V-8 with triple two-barrels—a *Six-Pack*—is available for the Plymouth Road Runner and the Dodge Super Bee.

1970—Chrysler begins to sell Mitsubishi cars and trucks in the United States. Hurst-modified Chrysler 300-H offered. Plymouth offers Duster coupe and the Road Runner Superbird "Winged Warrior." Plymouth Cricket imported from Britain.

1971—Chrysler buys share of Mitsubishi. Emission controls are expanded by the government. Last year for SIMCA. Last convertibles built.

1973—Rootes is now part of Chrysler. First OPEC oil crisis. Gas lines, and a shift in consumer priorities from miles per hour to miles per gallon.

1974—Barracuda discontinued.

1975—John J. Riccardo chairman, Eugene Cafiero president. Chrysler Cordoba debuts, Imperial discontinued.

1976—Aspen and Volare debut. Plymouth Arrow is imported from Mitsubishi.

1978—Lee A. Iacocca becomes president of financially troubled Chrysler Corporation. Four-wheel-drive Omni/Horizons introduced. Chrysler sells off European operations.

1979—Iacocca moves up to chairman, Paul Bergmoser becomes president.

1980—Guarantee Loan Act passed to bail out Chrysler Corporation. Marine Division sold. Chrysler sells fewer than 765,000 cars. The Imperial is briefly revived. Economy struggles and all U.S. automakers are in the red.

1981—K-car production begins. Defense Division sold. Gerald Greenwald vice chairman, Harold Sperlich president.

1982—Chrysler revives the convertible in the form of the Chrysler LeBaron.

1983—Loan guarantees paid off. Iacocca is in the spotlight. Minivan introduced. Last year for the slant six. A Shelby Charger is introduced.

1984—Chrysler buys part of Maserati. Daytona/Laser sport coupes introduced.

1985—Greenwald, chairman, Chrysler Motors; Bennett E. Bidwell, vice chairman, Chrysler Corp.; Harold Sperlich, president, Chrysler Motors. H Body Dodge Lancer and Chrysler LeBaron GTS Hatchbacks debut.

1986—7/70 warranty program introduced.

1987—Chrysler buys AMC and Lamborghini. Eagle introduced. Chrysler re-enters European market. Portofino show car introduced, precursor of the cab-forward designs. Robert S. Miller, vice chairman, Chrysler Corp.; Bidwell, president, marketing, Chrysler Motors; Robert A. Lutz, president, Chrysler Motors.

1988—Diamond Star, joint venture with Mitsubishi, begins. Greenwald, vice chairman, Chrysler Corp.; Miller, executive vice and chief financial officer, Chrysler Corp.; Bidwell, chairman, Chrysler Motors. Chrysler offers first airbags as standard equipment. Dodge Dynasty introduced.

1989—Chrysler signs agreement with Steyr-Daimler-Puch to build minivans in Europe. Maserati TC introduced. Last year for Reliant and Aries.

1990—Last year for Omni and Horizon, Viper Concept appears, first Talon/Laser.

1991—Robert Lutz is president, Chrysler Corp. Worst year ever for American Big Three. Chrysler sells share of Diamond Star. Chrysler Technical Center (CTC) in Auburn Hills, Michigan, dedicated.

1992—Jefferson North assembly plant opens; production of minivan begins in Europe. Dodge Viper introduced. LH cars debut. Robert J. Eaton, vice chairman, Chrysler Corp. Integrated child safety seats.

1993—Robert Eaton succeeds Lee Iacocca. Lutz becomes president. LH cars and Jeep Grand Cherokee debut. Last share in Mitsubishi sold.

1994—Thomas G. Denomme, vice chairman; Robert A. Lutz, vice chairman. First LHS models. Neon debuts.

1995—Cirrus and Stratus debut. Blue Ribbon emblem revived.

1996—Market share is 16.2 percent—highest since 1957. Minivans are redesigned. Prowler debuts. Sebring convertible debuts. New Chrysler Headquarters (CTC) in Auburn Hills, Michigan, officially opened.

1998—Chrysler merges with Daimler-Benz AG to make DaimlerChrysler, Juergen Shremp becomes chairman, Robert Eaton becomes vice chairman, Bob Lutz retires. Thomas Stallkamp, president, Chrysler Corp. New LH and LHS models, Durango SUV, 300M, and Grand Cherokee bow.

DAIMLER-BENZ

DAIMLER

1886—Gottlieb Daimler and Wilhelm Maybach build a two-wheeled gasoline
engined velocipede—the first motorcycle—and register for patent.
—Daimler and Maybach build a four-wheeled car with a high-speed
engine.

1889—Daimler and Maybach build a two-cylinder car.

1890—Daimler Motoren Gesellschaft established in Cannstadt.

1896—Daimler builds the first truck, a two-cylinder model with four
horsepower, and exports it to London.

1899—The Daimler Phoenix features a four-cylinder 10-horsepower engine.

1900—Gottlieb Daimler dies; Austrian distributor and board member Emil
Jellinek names a new Daimler model for daughter Mercedes.

1901—The first Mercedes model does a flying kilometer at more than 53
miles per hour. Heralded as the first modern motorcar.

1902—Mercedes name adopted and trademarked—and the first Mercedes
refined into the Simplex model.

1906–1909—Daimler establishes a U.S. subsidiary with Steinway, builds an
American Mercedes. Wilhelm Maybach resigns, succeeded by Paul
Daimler as chief engineer and designer. First marine diesel built. Three-
pointed star symbol adopted.

1910—Use of (American) Knight sleeve valve engine patent begun.
—Daimler Star registered as trademark.

1914—Mercedes 18/100 PS. The racing car that built the Silver Star legend,
and won the French Grand Prix three times, finishing 1-2-3 in 1914.

1918—First Daimler aircraft engine.

1922—Paul Daimler succeeded by Ferdinand Porsche as chief engineer and
designer. Porsche designs the "S" series cars.

1924—The Mercedes Targa Florio gets 150 horsepower from a 1,989-cc
supercharged engine.

BENZ

1883—Benz & Co. Rheinische Gasmotoren-Fabrik in Mannheim,
Germany, founded.

1886—Karl Benz receives a patent for a vehicle powered by a gas engine,
and a three-wheel velocipede is tested; the patent for it is considered the
"birth certificate of the automobile."

1893—Benz produces a four-wheeled car.

1894—The "Velo" is the world's first production car.

1895—Benz produces the first motor-driven truck.

1903—The "Parsifal" is the Benz answer to the Mercedes.

1908—Benz begins experimenting with diesels.

1909–1918—Laurel wreath insignia adopted. In a Benz dubbed *The*

Lightning, Barney Oldfield sets a 131-mile-per-hour land speed record;
Benz builds 3,000 cars.

1919—Benz exhibits diesel tractors.

1923—Tear-drop shaped ultralight "Tropfenwagen" racer astounds with
independent rear suspension and inboard rear brakes.

1924—Benz und Cie. enters into an agreement of mutual cooperation with
Daimler.

1926—Benz and Daimler merge to create Daimler-Benz AG.

DAIMLER-BENZ

1926–1929—Benz laurel surrounds Daimler star in new logo. Wilhelm Kissel
directs the new firm. The SSKL (built until 1934) can hit 140 miles per
hour with a six-cylinder supercharged engine; it wins its first race. Porsche
resigns and is succeeded by Hans Nibel as chief engineer and designer.
—Mercedes-Benz Stuttgart—first moderately priced car. Both Wilhelm
Maybach and Carl Benz die; 170 series debuts, features independent
front and rear suspension.

1934—Nibel dies, succeeded by Max Sailer. W25 racing car developed, the
W series will dominate racing until the war. 260 diesel car debuts.
Streamlined 320 model introduced.

1942—Kissel dies, is succeeded by Wilhelm Haspel; production shifts to
"jeep"-type vehicles, aircraft engines, and trucks.

1946—First postwar cars, the four-cylinder 170 V offered with either gas or
diesel engine.

1951—Six-cylinder 220 series.

1952—300 SL (Gullwing) coupe introduced as pace car; Daimler-Benz
concludes an agency agreement in the United States with Studebaker.

1953—180 series replaces 170; features monocoque construction.

1954—190SL—Four-cylinder roadster introduced as companion to more
expensive 300SL Gullwing coupe.

1964—600 series Pullman introduced.

1971—300SEL V-8 introduced.

1973—Foreign sales outstrip domestic; trucks are built in the United States.

1977—300 Turbo-diesel.

1981—Freightliner Truck in the United States acquired by Daimler-Benz.

1982—190 series bows.

1993—First cars assembled in Mexico.

1994—Work on Tuscaloosa, Alabama, plant begins; "Smart" minicar
announced as a joint venture.

1995—Juergen E. Shremp is chairman.

1997—U.S.-built M class debuts; Ford Heavy Diesel Truck Operations
purchased, renamed Sterling.

1998—Daimler-Benz AG merges with Chrysler Corporation in November
to create DaimlerChrysler.

INDEX